Italian Texts and Studies on Religion and Society

Edmondo Lupieri, *General Editor*

Italian religious history has been pivotal to the formation and growth of European and Western civilization and cultures. Unfortunately, many texts that are fundamental for the understanding of its importance have long remained inaccessible to non-Italian readers. Similarly, the exciting developments of Italian scholarship in the field of the studies of religion have not always come into the public eye outside of Italy. Particularly since the end of World War II there has been continuous expansion in the field, and currently Italian scholars are combining the old and solid Italian tradition of philological and historical studies with new and innovative ideas and methodologies.

Italian Texts and Studies on Religion and Society (ITSORS) is a new series. Its publications are all English translations of works originally published or composed in Italy. The main aim of ITSORS is to have readers in the English-speaking world become acquainted with Italian socio-religious history and with the best of Italian scholarly research on religion with socio-historical implications. For this reason ITSORS will have two branches: *Texts* and *Studies*.

Texts consist of classical works and are intended to be useful as sources for a better comprehension of important events in Western religious history. Many are not readily available or have never been translated into English. *Studies* comprise original works of the best contemporary Italian scholarship that offer methodological contributions to research and make inroads into seldom studied areas.

ITALIAN TEXTS
& STUDIES
ON RELIGION
& SOCIETY

BOOKS AVAILABLE

Odoric of Pordenone
The Travels of Friar Odoric
(Sponsored by the Chamber of Commerce of Pordenone, Italy)

Edmondo Lupieri
The Mandaeans: The Last Gnostics
(Sponsored by the Italian Ministry of Foreign Affairs)

Bruno Forte
The Essence of Christianity

The Essence of Christianity

BRUNO FORTE

Translated by
P. David Glenday

WILLIAM B. EERDMANS PUBLISHING COMPANY
GRAND RAPIDS, MICHIGAN / CAMBRIDGE, U.K.

© 2003 Wm. B. Eerdmans Publishing Co.
All rights reserved

Wm. B. Eerdmans Publishing Co.
255 Jefferson Ave. S.E., Grand Rapids, Michigan 49503 /
P.O. Box 163, Cambridge CB3 9PU U.K.

Printed in the United States of America

08 07 06 05 04 03   7 6 5 4 3 2 1

Library of Congress Cataloging-in-Publication Data

Forte, Bruno.
The essence of Christianity / Bruno Forte.
p.   cm.   — (Italian texts and studies on religion and society)
Includes bibliographical references and index.
ISBN 0-8028-2657-1 (pbk.)
1. Christianity — Essence, genius, nature. 2. Postmodernism —
Religious aspects — Christianity.   I. Title.   II. Series.

BT60.F67   2003
230 — dc22
2003062359

www.eerdmans.com

Contents

Contents

Foreword

B runo Forte, professor of dogmatics at the Pontifical Faculty of Theology in Naples and a member of the International Theological
Commission of the Holy See, is one of the most prolific, informed, cul-
turally aware, and spiritually sensitive theologians in Italy, and perhaps
even in the whole Catholic world. The present book results from a distinguished lectureship in Spain, at which the author was invited to state the
gist of his thought in brief compass.

In choosing to place this work under the title *The Essence of Christianity* Bruno Forte was aligning himself with a number of such enterprises
over the past two centuries. In an appendix to the book — which he teas-
ingly suggests readers might tackle first — Forte engages critically with a
number of his predecessors, some well known, some less so. Ludwig
Feuerbach heads the line, with *Das Wesen des Christentums* in 1841; but in
his reduction of theology to anthropology, making of God a self-
projection of humanity, Feuerbach ultimately descended into a solipsism
that did not even merit the name of an "unhappy love" that Karl Barth
found in Feuerbach for Christianity. Adolf von Harnack's Berlin lectures
of 1899-1900 located "das Wesen des Christentums" — which had
reached its apogee in German Protestantism — in a peaceable Kingdom
where the Fatherhood of God was matched by the brotherhood of all infinitely valuable human souls; but this expression of "tranquil love" between Christianity and modernity was soon in fact belied by the First
World War and the rest of the history of Europe in the "short century"
that began in 1914. Whether of the head or of the heart, whether idealist
or romantic, the subjectivity that marked both Feuerbach and Harnack

as men of the late Enlightenment was always headed for totalitarianism, says Forte, and when this in turn inevitably collapsed, the "will to power" had produced the nihilism that Nietzsche foresaw as its logical consequence. William Hamilton's "*New* Essence of Christianity" (1966), seeking to integrate "the death of God," proposed a life "without God or the confession of the Lord Jesus" and so, in effect, brought things back full circle to Feuerbach. More recently, some self-styled postmoderns have given up altogether on the search for truth and meaning; but the loss of transcendence leaves people dissatisfied. There are signs of "a rediscovery of the other," and even of "a longing for the Totally Other." In such a situation of crisis an opportunity arises for the gospel to be heard afresh. Bruno Forte writes in the service of that cause.

Among his predecessors Forte shows most sympathy for Romano Guardini, who, writing in 1938 under the shadow of totalitarianism, insisted on the concrete specificity of the revelation and redemption given from Beyond in the living person of Jesus Christ; from the viewpoint of "modern, emancipated rationality" the essence of Christianity could only appear as a "paradoxical love." Other twentieth-century theologians figuring positively in the background to Forte's thought are, in their respective and diverse ways, Karl Barth and Karl Rahner, Hans Urs von Balthasar and Eberhard Jüngel, although they receive little direct mention. More evident, though still not often cited, is Jürgen Moltmann with *Der gekreuzigte Gott* (1972) and *Trinität und Reich Gottes* (1980). For Forte, the epitome of Christianity is "crucified love."

Our author might have begun his own account with Ignatius of Antioch, echoes of whose language resound anonymously through this book. The second-century bishop and martyr spoke of Jesus Christ as "God's Word, who came forth out of the Silence into this world" (*Letter to the Magnesians*, 8.2), and "whoever truly possesses the word of Jesus is able to hear even its silence" (*Letter to the Ephesians*, 15.2). And a phrase from Ignatius's *Letter to the Romans* (7.2) was interpreted christologically by Origen to mean "My Love has been crucified." The human addressee of divine revelation and the beneficiary of redemption is identified by Forte in two familar quotations from St. Augustine: "Thou hast made us for Thyself, and our hearts are restless until they find their rest in Thee" (*Confessions*, I.1). As a result, humankind is confronted by the alternative: "Love of self till God is forgotten, or love of God till self is forgotten" (*City of God*, XIV.28).

Forte's account of the essence of Christianity is resolutely biblical, with the Scriptures being read in christological and trinitarian fashion in light of the great conciliar doctrines of Nicea, Constantinople, Ephesus, and Chalcedon. At the very heart of salvation history, for Forte, is the paschal mystery of Christ's Cross and Resurrection, which twentieth-century liturgical scholarship and compositions did much to restore as the central focus of the faith. Good Friday and Easter are given their trinitarian origin, character, and scope: the incarnate Son, at the end of a life lived in obedience to the Father (Matt. 4:1-11; 26:39; Heb. 5:7), at the moment of his dereliction on the Cross (Matt. 27:46), returns the Spirit to the Father (Luke 23:46), and receives the Spirit back at his Resurrection (Romans 1:4) — which he can then, on his own return to the Father, distribute to draw others into the divine life that his atoning work had rendered possible (Acts 2:33). The entire story is carried, according to Forte, by the humility of the loving and living God.

With an eye to contemporary searchers, Forte locates the beginning of faith in passionate questions about life and death and sees advancement as a struggle in encounter with the scandal of Christ's story. Our "human adventure" is best viewed as "a pilgrimage in search of the hidden Countenance," and what the gospel offers is a life of following Christ in the selfless way of freely obedient discipleship, and thus a grounded hope for eternity in the homeland. Keeping in mind the poet's declared intention to "make David speak like a Christian," anglophone churchgoers may aptly recall Isaac Watts's paraphrase of Psalm 90:

> Our God, our help in ages past,
> Our hope for years to come,
> Our shelter from the stormy blast,
> And our eternal home. . . .

It is "the communion of the Church" — Forte does not here broach the ecumenical question of where precisely that is to be found — that provides "the good news by which to respond to totalitarian violence and postmodern loneliness." The author ventures to formulate his own "ten commandments" — better, "moral injunctions" — to guide the conduct of believers and the Church(es) in the contemporary world.

Protestant readers especially, and perhaps some Northern Catholics, will marvel at the skill with which Forte — rather as Pope John Paul II toward the end of his 2003 encyclical reads the Eucharist in a Marian key — manages to discern and expound the mariological dimension of Christianity across its entire range. As Virgin, Mother, and Spouse, the Lady Mary is displayed as the willing cooperator of God in the accomplishment of his saving purpose for humankind and the cosmos. She is "Beauty in a fragment," and as such "an icon of the mystery of God" and a figure of the Church. All of this is of a piece, at the creaturely level, with the "motherly fatherhood" or "fatherly motherhood" of God, who is the Womb from which all things issue and to which they may return as participants in the Triune Life.

This is not to say that there are not (other) points also at which one might wish to discuss matters further with the author. For instance: whereas the Apostle Paul preached "first to the Jews" with a view to persuading them that Jesus was the Christ, Forte appears theologically content to envisage Church and Synagogue as continuing parallel — though mutually respectful — entities until the Parousia. Again: Forte follows some recent tendencies in Catholic theology, and indeed in magisterial teaching, to emphasize the "elements of truth and holiness" that may be found among other religious traditions and communities, but he says little about the transformation that they might undergo in being brought into captivity to Christ. Or yet again: when Forte transposes the impassibility and immutability of God into God's humble self-surrender and covenant faithfulness, it is not quite certain that everything important in the classical attributes is preserved in the switch from the metaphysical (God as "actus purus," as "semper agens") to the moral. Forte is, however, well aware that the Love that was crucified on Calvary is also, in the words of Forte's fellow countryman, "l'Amor che muove il sole e l'altre stelle," and it may be that what Forte calls "the dynamism of a living God" finds sufficient ontological grounding in Forte's perichoretic trinitarianism. Christianity is at stake in the recognition that the Incarnation and the Cross do not constitute God (as it might be in an Hegelian sense) but rather manifest him.

Bruno Forte and I will have things to talk about when next we meet. We first encountered each other in (I think) 1977, when we were somewhat younger theologians — he rather younger than I — at a consultation of the Conference of European Churches in Sofia, Bulgaria. We have since met on various ecclesiatical and academic occasions: in Budapest, in Oxford, even at Duke University. Meanwhile I am happy to commend to an American readership this stimulating work by an old friend.

GEOFFREY WAINWRIGHT
Durham, North Carolina
Feast of the Holy Cross 2003

Preface

The invitation to give Barcelona's "Aula Joan Maragall" 2002 — a short series of lectures in which to present what I consider most important in my books — reached me in the early months of 2000. At the time, which coincided with the Great Jubilee of the Incarnation, I was especially involved — both as a believer and as a theologian — in reflecting upon, and witnessing to, the centrality of Jesus Christ for every human life, and for the history of the world. So, in accepting the invitation, it was natural to think of proposing a course of lectures that focused on "the essence of Christianity."

I was immediately aware how demanding such an undertaking would be: by a remarkable coincidence, I would be working on my text exactly one hundred years after the evangelical theologian Adolf von Harnack had given his famous lectures with the same title to the students of Berlin University. I would also have to measure myself against the father of modern criticism of religion, and of Christianity in particular, Ludwig Feuerbach: in 1841 he had distilled his attack on theology and the Christian faith into a book entitled, precisely, "The Essence of Christianity."

Finally, I could not ignore the vigorous response offered to these two thinkers by the Catholic Romano Guardini, when in 1938 he had countered their critiques with his own interpretation of the heart of Christianity, in a text once again with exactly the same title. Guardini had written at a time when the barbarities of national socialism were in full flood, barbarities he himself resisted with all the strength and intelligence of his deep faith.

I was encouraged not to abandon the task by what was, at least apparently, a straightforward consideration, namely, that times have changed, and that if these three thinkers had responded to the question about Christianity's essence in the modern age, it would now fall to me to do this in the context of so-called postmodernity. I would thus have to define my approach beginning from theirs (and — not overly to weary my readers — I do this in the Appendix, which some will not read, others will read last, and others again — perhaps the most mischievous — will read first); I would have to clarify in broad lines what I understand by postmodernity; and, finally, I would have to seek briefly to present to this postmodern world what lies at the heart of Christianity, and why it seems to me that this may still be proposed as good news for the women and men of our time.

This is what I have sought to do in these pages, with the results that all will be able to judge for themselves. I am very much aware of this work's limitations, especially as I stand before the deep abyss that is the living God, for whose glory I accepted this challenge. On the other hand, and in any case, a few lectures cannot say everything: nor is the brevity required in such cases nec+essarily a bad thing.

So I am grateful to the Fundació Joan Maragall for the invitation to engage in this undertaking, and for having from the outset given it the nature of a service offered to the "global village," thanks to the condition they imposed of publishing the lectures in book form, first in Catalan and Spanish, and then in my own language, in which they were originally written.

B.F.

Where Are We? Who Are We?

You gave me the day, because you could only give me what you are.
Mother, you gave me the days of my death.
Since then, I live and die in you
who are love.
Since then, I am reborn from our death.

These lines — from *The Book of Questions* by Edmond Jabès[1] — show how, for us human beings, it is natural to struggle tirelessly against death, and how it is also just as natural for us to sense ourselves as mysteriously enfolded in our mother's womb, source of life without limit.

The weapon we wield in this combat is a question, the question which impels us beyond the threshold, and which alone is able to give us new birth, because it puts us strangely in touch with the maternal origin of all that lives. Our deepest identity as human beings, our indelible "name," is a question: "My name is a question, and I find freedom in my longing to ask questions."[2]

When we ask this question with passion, when we are genuinely interested in the answer, our hearts are made able to receive a revelation, we become capable of an encounter that transforms our very lives: we recognize our deep longing for a loving father-mother, who welcomes and cares for each one of us. Where, instead, thought alone tries to lord

1. E. Jabès, *Il libro delle interrogazioni*, 3rd ed. (Genova: Marietti, 1995), p. 61.
2. Jabès, *Il libro delle interrogazioni*, p. 103.

it over all, and the question simply becomes a way to dominate and do violence, we risk the shipwreck of an existence without moorings, and the anguish of a world with no origin or home.

In the landscape of time and of the heart, this loving father-mother is a decisive point of reference, against which we can discern the meaning, and the success or failure, of our human adventure. Towards this figure the great religions converge, and also precisely in relation to it they show how different they are. To take this figure as a key for a reading of modernity and its crisis will help us to answer the double, decisive question: Where are we? and who are we?

Landscape of Our Times

Modernity's Dream — and the "Murder of the Father"

The metaphor of light provides us with the most eloquently expressive way of talking about the principle that inspired modernity — adult reason's ambitious claim of understanding and mastering everything. This project — which lay at the foundations of the Enlightenment in all its manifestations — maintains that to understand the world rationally means to make human beings free at last, masters and captains of their own future, emancipating them from every possible dependence.

"Emancipation": this was the dream that pervaded the great processes of historical transformation in the modern age, born with the "age of lights" and the French Revolution: from the emancipation of the exploited classes, the oppressed races, and the peoples of the so-called "third world" to the liberation of women, in all the variety of the different cultural and social contexts.

This dream of total emancipation strained forward towards a reality entirely illuminated by the idea as such, where the power of reason may express itself without constraint. As Hegel wrote so emphatically: "Never since the sun had stood in the firmament and the planets revolved around him had it been perceived that man's existence centers in his head, *i.e.*, in Thought, inspired by which he builds up the world of reality. . . [N]ot until now had man advanced to the recognition of the principle that thought ought to govern spiritual reality. This was accordingly a glorious mental dawn."[3] Where reason triumphs, there rises the sun of the future; in this sense, it may be said that modernity is the age of light. This heady modern spirit lies behind claims that absolute reason can vanquish every shadow and resolve every difference. . . .

The fullest expression of this spirit is "ideology": modernity, the age that dreamt of emancipation, was also the time of those all-embracing ways of understanding the world proper of the ideologies. Ideologies tend to impose the light of reason on the whole of reality, to the point of equating ideal and real. In pursuit of this ambition, the "great ideological narratives" tended to construct a "society without fathers," where there are no vertical relationships — held unfailingly to imply dependence — but only horizontal ones, of equality and reciprocity.

The sun of reason generates liberty and equality, and hence fraternity, in an egalitarianism founded on the one light of thought, which governs the whole world and all life: "liberté, égalité, fraternité" are the sweet fruits of reason's triumph. The critique of the "father-lord" figure thus leads to the complete rejection of God. Just as on earth there must be no fatherhood creating dependence, so in heaven there may be no Father of all.

There are no divine "partners," there is no other world; there is only this history, this horizon. The only idea of God allowed to stand before the court of adult reason is of a God who is dead, meaningless, and with no practical purpose ("Deus mortuus, Deus otiosus"). This collective murder of the Father is carried out in the conviction that human beings must manage their own lives for themselves, molding their destiny with their own hands. The modern ideologies, whether of right or left, pursued this ambitious aim of emancipating the dwellers in time in a way so radical as to make them the sole object and subject of their history, and at the same time both the source and goal of all that happens.

There can be no denying that this is a mighty project, and that we are all in some measure its debtors: Who would want to live in a society that had not undergone this process of emancipation? And yet, this dream has also led to satanic consequences: precisely because of its all-embracing ambition, ideology becomes violent. Reality is forced to bend to the idea;

---

3. G. W. F. Hegel, *The Philosophy of History*, trans. J. Sibree (Kitchenor, Ont.: Batoche Books, 2001), pp. 466-67.

reason's "will to power" (F. Nietzsche) strives to dominate life and history so as to make them conform to its own ends.

Inexorably, this all-encompassing dream becomes totalitarian: totality — as understood by reason — produces totalitarianism. Neither by chance nor accident, all the enterprises of modern ideology, of right and left, bourgeois and revolutionary, eventually issue in totalitarian and violent expression. And it is precisely this historical experience of totalitarianism that leads to the crisis and twilight of the claims of modern reason: "The enlightenment, in its fullest sense as thought in continuous progress," affirm Max Horkheimer and Theodor W. Adorno at the beginning of their *Dialectic of the Enlightenment,* "has always aimed at freeing men from fear and making them their own masters. But the fully enlightened earth radiates disaster triumphant."[4]

Thought without shadows becomes tragedy; far from emancipating, it generates suffering, alienation, and death. The modern "society without fathers" does not bear children who are freer and more equal, but, instead, dramatic dependencies on those who at various times offer themselves as "surrogate" fathers. The "leader," the "party," the "cause," these become the new masters, and the freedom promised and dreamt of turns into a painful, gray manipulation of the masses, held in place by violence and fear. The collective murder of the father did not prevent this proliferation of these new, barely camouflaged "fathers" and "lords." . . .

A Society without Fathers and the "Short Century"

The dream of emancipating life and the world seems, then, to have dashed itself against the unheard-of violence produced by the age of emancipation. Eloquent witnesses to this are the wars, ethnic cleansings, crematory ovens, the Shoah and genocides of the last century, as well as the massacre caused by hunger every day in the world. Are these the fruits of adult reason? Where are the new heavens and new earth promised by the great ideological narratives?

This is the drama with which the twentieth century closed: a moral

---

4. M. Horkheimer and Th. W. Adorno, *Dialectic of the Enlightenment* (1944; New York, 1969), p. 3.

drama, a crisis of meaning, a vacuum of hope. If, for modern reason, everything found meaning within one all-encompassing process, for the "weak thought" of the postmodern condition — shipwrecked on the great sea of history after the collapse of ideology's claims — nothing seems to have meaning anymore. In reaction to the failed claims of "strong" reason, then, there emerge the contours of a time of shipwreck and collapse; this crisis of meaning is the special characteristic of postmodern restlessness. In this "night of the world" (Martin Heidegger), what seems to triumph is indifference, a loss of the taste for seeking ultimate reasons for human living and dying. And thus, too, we reach the nadir of the century that has not long ended, that is, nihilism.

Nihilism is not simply a matter of giving up values for which it is worth living, but a more subtle process: it deprives human beings of the taste for committing themselves to a higher cause, of those powerful motivations that the ideologies still seemed to offer. Our worst contemporary ailment is this lack of "passion for the truth": this is the tragic face of our postmodern age. In this climate of diffuse nihilism, everything conspires to lead us not to think anymore, to flee from any passionate striving after truth, to abandon ourselves instead to whatever may be enjoyed at once, its value calculated only by the interest in immediate consumption.

This is the triumph of the mask over truth: even the very values themselves are often reduced to banners hoisted to camouflage the lack of real meaning. Human beings seem to be reduced to a "useless passion" (the expression used, disturbingly ahead of the times, by Jean-Paul Sartre: "l'homme, une passion inutile"). One could say that the most serious malady of this so-called postmodern age is the definitive abandonment of the search for a father-mother towards whom to hold out our arms, our no longer having the will or desire to seek a meaning worth living and dying for.

Orphaned by the ideologies, we all run the risk of being more fragile, more tempted to shut ourselves up in the loneliness of our own selfishness. This is why post-ideological societies are increasingly becoming "collections of solitudes" in which people seek their own self-interest, defined according to an exclusively selfish and manipulative logic: faced with the vacuum of ultimate meaning, we grasp at penultimate concerns, and seek immediate possession.

This explains the triumph of the most shameless consumerism, of the rush towards hedonism and whatever may be enjoyed at once; but this is also the deep reason for the emergence and affirmation of forms of thought that are sectarian, narrowly ethnic, nationalistic, or regional, and that spread with alarming virulence throughout Europe at the end of the last century. Without the wide horizons offered by truth, we easily drown in the selfish loneliness of our own particular situation, and our societies become archipelagos, collections of separate islands.

Yet it is exactly this process which shows that we all need a common father-mother to free us from the confines of our selfishness, to offer a horizon for which to hope and love — not the claustrophobic, violent horizon of the ideologies, but one that truly frees all, and respects all. So if the "society without fathers" ran after the dream of emancipation, and to achieve this dream sought to destroy the father, it is precisely the bitter fruit of totalitarian and violent emancipation — and the vacuum it created — that evokes the newly felt need for a father-mother who welcomes us in freedom and love. This is certainly not to seek a father-mother whose place could be taken by the party, or the boss, or unquestioned leaders, or money, or capitalism; it is, rather, the longing for a father-mother who, at one and the same time, founds the dignity of each person, the freedom of all, and the meaning of life.

In short, faced with the indifference and lack of passion for the truth that characterize our present age, our greatest need is to discover the countenance of the father-mother who loves us. It is our longing for the Totally Other, of whom Horkheimer and Adorno spoke as they foresaw the crisis of the ideologies. It is the yearning for the hidden Face, the need for a home to be shared, which provides horizons of meaning without violence.

This is what emerges from the whole arc traced by the modern age: from the triumph of reason in the Enlightenment, which sought to embrace and explain everything with reason's light alone, to the more diffuse experience of fragmentation and nonsense that followed upon the collapse of the mighty horizons of ideology. This is the process that characterized the twentieth century, the so-called "short century" ("the Short Twentieth Century": Eric Hobsbawm),[5] marked by both the triumph and crisis of the totalitarian optimism of the various ideological models.

5. E. J. Hobsbawm, *The Age of Extremes: A History of the World, 1914-1991* (New York: Vintage Books, 1996), p. 22.

The continuing violence, the ethnic hatreds, the blind prejudices against everything different, show how we may have sung too soon the "requiem" of the ideologies, and how they have taken their revenge by reappearing with all the virulence of their mechanisms of self-justification and of demonization of the other: in the suffering inflicted on defenseless peoples, in genocide, in the vicious propaganda of opposing parties, in the vendettas of terrorism. The metaphor of the night really does seem the least inadequate to describe our present condition, notwithstanding the ideologies' renewed claims of being able to understand everything by the "light" of reason alone.

And yet, paradoxically, it is precisely from this continuing and evident denial of fraternity among human beings that there rises up all the more loudly the cry of need for a rediscovered brotherhood, for which only a father-mother can provide the foundation. There are signs of expectation: there is a "longing for perfect and achieved justice" (Max Horkheimer), which can be perceived in the contemporary restlessness and "search for lost meaning." This is not simply "une recherche du temps perdu," not mere nostalgia, but a striving to rediscover meaning beyond shipwreck, to make out an ultimate horizon against which to measure all that is penultimate, and to give an ethical foundation to what we do.

There is a *rediscovery of the other*, in the recognition that my neighbor, by the mere fact of existing, can give me a reason to live, because he or she challenges me to go out of myself, to take the risk of the exodus with no return involved in committing myself in love to others. The new concern for the weakest — especially for foreigners fleeing from situations of deprivation and poverty of every kind — and the growing awareness of the demands of local and global solidarity may be counted — even if still in the midst of many contradictions — as signs of this search for lost meaning.

At the same time, there seems also to be a rediscovery of the longing for the Totally Other, a kind of *rediscovery of the sacred* over against every nihilistic denial. There is the reawakening of a need, which may be described in general as religious: for an ultimate horizon, a home, but not in the manipulative and violent way of ideology. Under very different forms, there is a "return to the Father," even though not always without ambiguity or even a certain ideological nostalgia.

In fact, if the crisis of the modern age marks the end of the claims of the absolute subject, the signs that its time is over — beyond nihilism — all point in the direction of a rediscovery of the Other, able to offer reasons for life and hope. The Second Vatican Council expressed this intuition in a particularly deep way when it said: "One is entitled to think that the future of humanity is in the hands of those who are capable of providing the generations to come with reasons for life and optimism" (*Gaudium et Spes* 31). In these words we can espy the role of a fundamental paternal-maternal mediation, of a kind of paternity-maternity of meaning, which might be able to stop the future from falling into nothingness and its seductive power. The Other — ultimate foundation of all real reasons to live, and to live together — seems to be offering himself as the answer to the truest and deepest question revealed by the crisis of our present age; and the yearning for his hidden face seems to lead us towards a father-mother who has a loving welcome for us all. . . .

Landscape of Our Hearts

"Impelled towards Death," or Open to Mystery

The question living deep in our hearts, making us restless and thoughtful, is about the world's great suffering; it is the unavoidable question of death and the end of everything. If there were no death, there would be no thought; everything would be a flat eternity, at least for our limited speculative capacities. In this sense, to live is to learn to die, to learn how to live with the silent, persistent, and unyielding challenge of death.

It is futile, with the Epicureans, to seek escape or facile consolation: "When death comes, I will no longer exist, and as long as I exist, there is no death." These words are a fraud, a charade, because death is not only a destiny that awaits us at the end, but it is above all a presence looming over every day of our fragile, weak lives. "Death," writes Martin Heidegger, "is not something not yet present-at-hand, nor is it that which is ultimately still outstanding but which has been reduced to a minimum. *Death is something that stands before us — something impending.*"[6] Different

6. M. Heidegger, *Being and Time*, trans. John Macquarrie and Edward Robinson (New York: Harper, 1962), §50, pp. 293-94.

by birth, opportunity, and experience, we dwellers in time are one in our poverty, because we are all "impelled" in the same direction, towards death, inexorably turned towards the "last frontier," enfolded in silence:

> We do not know what will be our lot
> tomorrow, whether in shadow or joy;
> perhaps our path
> will lead to who knows what pastures
> where youth's eternal waters murmur;
> or maybe it will wind down
> to the last frontier,
> in the dark, with the morning forgotten.[7]

Life seems to come down to no more than a journey inexorably bound for darkness, and so our struggle to exist is full of sadness, and we dwell in time as if plunged into the abyss of nothingness. It is there, on the threshold of this nothingness that we experience anguish: suspended over the silent depths of death, we are restless about what awaits us. Our repugnance before nothingness provokes a reaction in us — the ability to ask questions: indeed, we become a question to ourselves, and paths seem to open up for us, towards what might, or will never, be.

Like a faithful, lifelong companion, we carry within us the question — avoided or welcomed, hidden or sought — that death inflicts like a wound in the very depths of our hearts. So it is that thought is born from death, and consciousness from the passionate longing of those who are not ready to resign themselves to the final triumph of nothingness: "All cognition of the All originates in death, in the fear of death," writes Franz Rosenzweig. Philosophy takes it upon itself to throw off the fear of things earthly, to rob death of its poisonous sting, and Hades of its pestilential breath. "All that is mortal lives in this fear of death; every new birth augments the fear by one new reason, for it augments what is mortal. . . . But philosophy denies these fears of the earth. It bears us over the grave which yawns at our feet with every step. It lets the body be a prey to the abyss, but the free soul flutters away over it."[8]

7. E. Montale, *Ossi di seppia, Mediterraneo,* in *Tutte le poesie* (Milano: Mondadori, 1984), p. 58.

8. F. Rosenzweig, *The Star of Redemption* (Notre Dame: University of Notre Dame Press, 1985), p. 3.

Our struggle against death finds expression in the questions born in our heart — unexpected, sudden — like aching wounds: What is to become of me? What does my life mean? Where I am bound, with my baggage of pain, consolation, and joy? And when I have finally attained what I desire, what else will I long for, if not final victory, victory over death? When we consider the lowest point towards which we are bound, it is precisely there that we discover how we struggle to overturn death's apparent triumph.

Precisely the fact that death makes us think, and that we sense the need to give meaning to our days and deeds, shows that deep in our hearts we pilgrims towards death are in reality called to life. Deep in our hearts we encounter an indestructible longing for Someone's face, someone who will receive our suffering and tears, and who can redeem the endless sorrow of our days.

When we are alone or in despair, when no one seems to want us anymore, and when we have good reason even to despise or regret who we are, then it is that we discover within us the yearning for another, one who is ready to welcome us, and make us feel loved beyond everything, in spite of everything, conquering the last enemy who is death. This is exactly what Augustine says as he begins his *Confessions*: "Fecisti cor nostrum ad te et inquietum est cor nostrum donec requiescat in te" — "You have made our heart for You, and our heart is restless until it rests in You."

In the question each of us bears deep in our hearts we find the face of a loving father-mother, a metaphor of our need for someone to whom we can entrust ourselves unconditionally, an anchor, a harbor where there is rest for our weariness and sorrow, where we are certain that we will not be sent back to the abyss of nothingness. This need for the other, for the father-mother who welcomes us, this deep longing, each one of us can recognize within, if only we have the courage not to hide behind our pretensions to greatness, or to retreat behind our defenses. Thus understood, the figure of the loving father-mother is the womb, the home, the origin where all that we are can find rest. If deep in our hearts we are all inhabited by the anguish of the ultimate challenge of death, and if this makes us stop and think, then the image of this paternal, maternal, welcoming love is what best responds to what we all infinitely need.

Rejecting — and Expecting — the Father

We cannot then but wonder: If all this is true, why do so many of us experience such a visceral rejection of the father-figure? Why, sooner or later in life, do we all experience a time of protest against the image of the father-mother?

Perhaps some light may be thrown on this obvious contradiction between our need to be accepted and so overcome anguish, and our rejection of this need, by looking deeper into the human heart. We might take, for example, a letter written to his father by Franz Kafka, one of the greatest witnesses to the restlessness of our times: "The sensation of nothingness which often overwhelms me originates in great part in your influence over me. . . . I have been able to enjoy what you gave us only at the cost of shame, effort, weakness, and a sense of guilt. I could only show you my gratitude like a beggar, not by deeds. The first visible result of this education was that it made me flee from everything that, even distantly, reminded me of you."[9] How often the rejection of the father is born from this need not to be dependent! And how often fatherhood turns into possessiveness, slavery, and domination! Here, too, we encounter the roots of what has dramatically been called the "murder of the father."

This "murder" is a sort of ritual gesture, intended to affirm our independence and autonomy. It is inseparable from a sense of anguish: but if one of the deep causes of this anguish is the approach of death, to eliminate the father-mother figure who will receive us means exposing ourselves even more completely to the clutches of nothingness. It is like becoming orphans, and as a result we experience even more acutely the longing for the father and mother who would welcome us in love.

From this there arises paradoxical behavior: on the one hand, we flee from the father-mother figure, to be free and independent like the prodigal son, who chose to take his inheritance and manage his own life; on the other, there grows stronger in us the aching need for someone who will show us the face of a loving father-mother without making us feel like slaves. The human heart is truly an abyss, and the weight of its contradictions can tear it apart.

9. F. Kafka, *Lettera al Padre* (November 1919), 11th ed. (Milano: Feltrinelli, 2001), pp. 14 and 32f.

A father-mother who loves us and sets us free is someone who does not compete with our freedom, but rather gives that freedom its foundation, the ultimate guarantee of the truth and peace of our hearts; someone who heals our anguish with the medicine of love, but who also heals the fear we have of losing our freedom, by leading us to feel loved in a way that does not make us dependent. It is such a motherly father that the human heart needs, longing as we do for a womb that enfolds and guards us, and generates us unceasingly to life.

This longing is expressed with moving intensity by one of the most representative figures of the "short century": Edith Stein. Philosopher, student and colleague of Husserl, daughter of Israel, witness in solidarity of the greatest tragedy of her people, in love with Christ, formed in "the knowledge of the Cross," this exceptional woman, who gazed into the human heart like few others, writes:

> Who are you, sweet light, that fills me
> And illumines the darkness of my heart?
> You lead me like a mother's hand,
> And should you let go of me,
> I would not know how to take another step.
> You are the space
> That embraces my being and buries it in yourself.
> Away from you it sinks into the abyss
> Of nothingness, from which you raised it to the light.
> You, nearer to me than I to myself,
> And more interior than my most interior
> And still impalpable and intangible
> And beyond any name:
> Holy Spirit eternal love.[10]

The choice these words indicate is urgent and decisive — between living like pilgrims in search of the hidden Countenance, letting ourselves be guided by the fatherly-motherly hand of the Other, or shutting ourselves up in our fears and loneliness. Life is either a pilgrimage, or a foretaste of death. It is either passion, search, and restlessness, or it is letting ourselves die a little each day, escaping in all the ways our society makes possible, and that help us be distracted and not ask the real questions. A

10. "Novena of the Holy Spirit," by E. Stein (St. Benedicta of the Cross).

decision must be made: "I will arise and go to my father!" We have to open ourselves to listen and cry out. This is the most necessary choice for the women and men of this postmodern age.

To help their companions take this step, believers will have to be the first to arise and go to the Father, becoming pilgrims again, overcoming the weariness and frustration that sometimes take hold of them, especially when results seem not to come. Believers know they are not in this world to see the harvest, but to plant the seed. As Luther affirmed, "Even if I knew the world would end tomorrow, I would not hesitate to plant a seed today." For those who believe in God, what is important is not the harvest, but the sowing: the fruit will come when and how God wills. Thus it is that our "no" to frustration must be joined to our "yes" to the passion for truth that stirs up the real questions in the hearts of human beings, and leads them to seek the hidden Countenance, the face of the loving father-mother, which is the meaning of life, and the hope of the world. . . .

When Religions Meet

Faced with the mystery of the world, seeking and hoping for a loving father-mother of all, Christianity has much in common with humanity's other religious experiences. Dialogue with these world religions is all the more necessary and urgent now that the "global village" draws believers together, and calls them to unite and serve the unity of the human family.

Nevertheless, this encounter between religions must never mean for anyone, much less for Christians, giving up the truth to which they mean to offer obedience. Consequently, to reflect on the relationship between Christianity and the great world religions — beginning from the foundational and unique relationship with the faith of Israel, to that with the other great monotheistic religion, Islam, and finally with the other world religions — will be of no little help in identifying the "essence of Christianity" which we seek.

Judaism and Christianity

In the Land promised to the fathers, Judaism today is able again to express itself in the full variety of its forms. Also as a result of this decisive new factor, as well as of the tragic events of the "Shoah" — the enormous catastrophe which raised with unheard-of seriousness the question of the relationship between the God of the Bible and the suffering of his children, and which has inspired a new sensibility regarding the responsibilities of Christians for anti-Semitism — the relationship between Christianity and the Hebrew faith has become the object of new awareness among Christians.

This awareness has its roots, on the one hand, in the importance of the final gathering of Israel, for which Jesus gave his life, and, on the other, in the apostle Paul's reading of the great "mystery" by which this glorious gathering is delayed in time (cf. Rom. 9:11). Israel and the church walk together towards the fulfillment of God's promises, when — again according to Paul — the two peoples will be fully reconciled, in a way that can be compared to a true "resurrection of the dead" (Rom. 11:15).

This means that, in the intermediate period between the first and second comings of the Lord Jesus, what Jews and Christians can and must seek is a path towards reconciliation, more than the reconciliation already achieved: this last will be granted at the time which the God of the promise has reserved for his creatures. This clarification frees us at once from hazardous expectations: whatever paths individuals may choose to follow, according to the particular plans of the Eternal God for each person, Israel and the church will have to walk not confused, even if inseparable, till the final reconciliation worked by the Lord — the eschatological "shalom," the fully achieved kingdom of God, which is the messianic hope of both peoples.

This idea of a reconciliation in the making transcends every theory of substitution, by which the church has simply taken Israel's place in the divine plan of salvation: it is Paul himself who warns against rendering vain what he calls the "mystery" (Rom. 11:25), on the basis of which Israel — inasmuch as she maintains the faith of the fathers — remains the witness of the election and promises of God, and offers herself to the church as the "holy root" (cf. Rom. 11:26 and 18) on which the church is grafted, and from which it will never be legitimate for her to depart.

In the one great plan of salvation, there is the people of the covenant, which has never been withdrawn, even if it is still not fully achieved, and there is the church, the people established in the covenant made in the blood of Christ. The plan of salvation is one, but the covenants are different: from that with Noah, to that with Abraham and the patriarchs, from that with Moses to that established in the death and resurrection of the Lord Jesus. The fundamental structure of the relationship created by revelation — by which the Eternal has given himself in love to his people, and this people is called to give itself in faith to him — is one, but the stages and forms of the divine plan for history are several.

There will, therefore, be no authentic process of reconciliation between the church and Israel without the recognition of the irreplaceable value of the "holy root," and therefore without the effective love of Christians for the promise made to the fathers, the writings in which this is expressed, and the people who have been — and are — its witnesses in history at the cost even of their lives. Yet neither would the journey of reconciliation be authentic, if it excluded for Christians the confession of Jesus as Lord and Christ, a confession offered in word and deed to him who is the stone of scandal placed in Zion, in the conviction that "whoever believes in him will not be put to shame" (Rom. 9:33).

The two peoples must thus walk together towards the same goal, but the church, recognizing Israel as the root that precedes and earths it, cannot but look to Israel and the future of the promise through the revelation of the Lord Jesus. This idea is expressed by the beautiful patristic image, taken from the scriptures, of the explorers sent by Moses into the land of Canaan, who "came to the Wadi Eshcol, and cut down from there a branch with a single cluster of grapes, and they carried it on a pole between the two of them" (Num. 13:23), to show it to the people and set them alight with the desire for conquest. In the wood from which hang the grapes the fathers recognized the cross on which hangs Christ.[11] In the two pole-bearers, instead, they saw the church and Israel, both looking towards the same destination, united by the same hope. Their difference lies in the fact that while Israel sees ahead of it an open horizon, the church, which follows, looks to the same horizon, but does this through the grapes and the wood of the pole, as well as through the one who precedes — through, that is, the crucified Lord and the people of the covenant which has never been revoked.[12] To walk in

11. "Figura Christi pendentis in ligno" — "Figure of Christ hanged on the wood": Evagrius, *Altercatio inter Theophilum et Simonem,* PL 20:1175.

12. "Subvectantes phalanguam, duorum populorum figuram ostendebant, unum priorem, scilicet vestrum, terga Christum dantem, alium posteriorem, racemum respicientem, scilicet noster populus intelligitur" — "The bearers of the rod showed forth the figure of the two peoples, the one, that in front, yours, with its back to Christ, the other, behind and looking towards the grapes, ours": Evagrius, *Altercatio,* PL 20:1175.

step, even if in difference, is therefore the task to be accomplished in view of the final reconciliation: this requires from the disciples of Jesus, in particular, to join their confession of him to a love for Israel, even if in the awareness of a duality, and even of a hiatus, which cannot be ignored, and which must be lived in mutual respect, in common witness to the one God and in expectation of the fulfillment of his promises.

It is evident that the relationship between Judaism and Christianity has not always been understood and lived like this: indeed, history abounds with the prejudices and misunderstandings of Christians towards the Hebrew people. That is why, for progress to be made along the path of reconciliation, we will need "teshuva," a Hebrew word that means "return," "conversion." And this at various levels: in the first place, we need to identify with clarity, and accept, the faults committed against the Hebrew people and those who were in fact responsible for them. This must be done not only for the "Shoah," but also more generally in relation to the "teaching of scorn" that underpinned so much anti-Semitism and so much of the chosen people's suffering.

However, an overly generalized admission of guilt risks placing responsibility on so many as to be vague. We should, rather, confess the faults actually committed, asking all concerned to demonstrate that greatness of heart which makes it possible to ask forgiveness also in the name of those who were in fact guilty of the events of the Shoah, which took place in Christian Europe. This magnanimity will have also to extend to all the holocausts for which the human family has been responsible, even in more recent times: the firm condemnation of anti-Semitism must go hand in hand with a deeper sensitivity towards all forms of violations of human rights, in the interests of effective solidarity with the defeated and oppressed.

This attitude of "teshuva" is also required from the Jewish people with respect to the historical responsibilities that fall to them, especially today: precisely thus will they be able to demonstrate the excellence of their election, and the unique mercy of the Lord which they have experienced, so as to be witnesses to the one God, the father-mother of all, together with the disciples of Jesus, a Jew and a Jew forever.

Christianity and Islam

When Christians reflect on their relationship with Islam, they must begin from an appreciation of the good produced by the faith in the one God taught by Mohammed: "We must never forget the great power for good that Islam represents for the majority of its adherents. . . . Millions of Muslims, in their humble submission to God's will, in their faithful observance of the prescriptions of the law, in their daily exercise of the virtues of patience, of mutual help, and of acceptance of suffering, find a moral strength which allows them to respond here on earth to their vocation as religious persons. This is Islam's greatness, and makes that faith one of humanity's great moral powers."[13]

This appreciation, however, must not be allowed to obscure the real differences between Christianity and Islam, and, even less, how difficult life can be for Christians living in an Islamic environment: "Wherever Islam is the State religion, minorities are subjected to social pressure and are continuously and unremittingly eroded."[14] This fact is inseparable from what essentially differentiates the two faiths: "Mahomet slew; Jesus Christ caused His own to be slain," says Pascal; "Mahomet took the way to succeed from a worldly point of view, Jesus Christ, from the same point of view, took the way to perish."[15]

Even if Pascal's observation seems brutal, it does contain a basic truth: at the heart of Jesus' gospel there is love, understood not only as the revelation of God's countenance, but also as a priority task vis-à-vis one's neighbor. It is this love, understood as the freely offered, unconditional gift of self, which is, instead, missing from the ninety-nine names of God professed by Islam, and which, when it appears in the later Islamic mystical texts, has clearly identifiable Christian roots.

One can thus explain the difference by which the one God — worshiped by both religions — is considered by Islam, on the one hand, as entirely other and sovereign, even if merciful and faithful, and by Christianity as the Trinitarian God, in his very self the communion that exists between eternal Lover, eternally Beloved, and eternal Love. Naturally, it is not enough to proclaim that God is love to live in love: the historical

---

13. G. Anawati, *Islam e Cristianesimo* (Milano: Vita e Pensiero, 1994), p. 15.
14. G. Anawati, *Islam e Cristianesimo* p. 13.
15. *Pensées*, trans. W. F. Trotter (New York: E. P. Dutton, 1948), no. 598, p. 165.

failings of Christians are evident proof of this; and the church, in acknowledging these failings, does so precisely in order to obey the truth of the gospel and grow in love.

The blood that Christians were instrumental in spilling, or the counter-witness they offered to the gospel, is no less serious than the violence exercised by Muslims, or the selfishness of some of their moral choices. Made one by the fact that their followers fail, the two creeds nevertheless continue to be different as just explained, and this is far from irrelevant: "holy war" in the name of Allah will always be an exemplary possibility for Muslims; violence exercised in the name of the gospel will always remain a scandal and a contradiction of that gospel, a betrayal that, for all the many times it has been perpetrated in history, will nonetheless always be condemned by Christians fully aware of the gospel's demands.

This difference concerning the central content of the faith also implies a different way of understanding the way God communicates himself: for Christianity, revelation happens through events and words, to which the inspired text bears witness, without, though, saying everything there is to say about the riches contained in those events and words. That is why the sacred scriptures in the Judeo-Christian tradition require interpretation, the task of digging deeper to seek understanding of the depths of the mystery to which the "letter" (always treated with respect) opens the way. It is no accident that hermeneutics as the science of interpretation was born within the Judeo-Christian exegesis of revelation!

With Islam it is otherwise: the Prophet writes down what is dictated to him, and his text is so sacred and untouchable that it can only be applied and obediently repeated, but never interpreted as such. There is in Islam such an authority of the inspired text that, if on the one hand that text is the object of respect and obedience, it can also, on the other, generate a fundamentalist kind of adherence, and cause the Prophet's teaching to become above all a code of laws.

For the Bible, interpretation is necessary at all levels, and opens up wide areas of freedom, with the possibility of penetrating ever more deeply into the meaning of the texts. In Islam, recourse to the inspired text can tend to reassure believers that they possess the truth, and can thus generate a fundamentalism in application that may reach the extremes of intolerance towards what is different and the denial of religious freedom.

We are thus brought to that complex of questions which more than anything else fire the debate on the new presence of Islam in many countries of ancient Christian tradition: foreseeing an exponential growth in this presence, should we fear for religious freedom, and for democracy, in cultures used to democratic liberties, with a strong awareness — derived from Christianity — of the inalienable value of the person and his/her rights? The answer is neither simple nor straightforward: both those who raise the alarm, and those who call for respect for the other and acceptance of difference, have their good reasons.

Throughout its history, Islam has found various "modus vivendi," above all in the matter of coexistence with Christianity and Judaism, religions of the Book tolerated because of a shared ancestry in the father of believers, Abraham. Yet the formula of "tolerance" — where it has been applied — has involved the obligation to acquire this right, a tax to be paid (the "capitation": — *izya*). Who — in cultures that have passed through the modern process of emancipation — could accept the legitimacy of such a principle? Is not freedom of conscience, and in particular religious liberty, an inalienable right of every person?

If to this we add the examples — available, unfortunately, up till the present in various Islamic countries — of a real persecution of what is different, of the denial of the right to conversion from Islam to any other religious persuasion whatever, of the limitations placed upon the liberties of large social groups, beginning with women, one can understand that the concerns raised are worthy of the utmost consideration. It is certainly not a matter of denying the value of dialogue, based on truth and on respect for each person; nor can there be a demand for policies of rejection or exclusion, aimed at protecting the Christian identity against possible dangers (if this identity is alive and vital, it will be its own protection!).

What, instead, may legitimately be sought is a double, necessary guarantee: on the one hand, that respect for the identity of each individual may be expressed not only towards the new arrivals, but also towards those who welcome them, such that the rights and liberties of all are guaranteed and promoted; and, on the other, that the respect and liberty accorded to the adherents of Islam in the countries of Christian tradition be analogously offered to followers of the other religions, and to nonbelievers, in Islamic countries.

Without this reciprocity doubts will persist as to whether it is really possible for these two religions, so close to each other and yet so distant, to live in peaceful coexistence. As long as even a single Muslim is deprived of his/her civil rights, or of his/her very life, because of being converted to the gospel, and as long as Christians continue to be persecuted in Islamic countries, concern regarding the encounter between Islam and cultures characterized by Christianity will be more than legitimate.

The challenge, then, is directed above all to Muslims, so that what they seek for themselves should be guaranteed to everyone in the countries they come from, and thus also to Christians, so that, while the latter respect the identity of those who are different from them, they also do not fail to proclaim to all the riches of the gospel and the salvation it offers.

Christianity and the Other World Religions

From India and the Far East, Christianity is challenged by Asia's great religions: especially because of immigration to the West, which has increased in recent decades, but also because distances have shrunk owing to globalization, these religions (Hinduism, Buddhism, Taoism, Confucianism, Shintoism) are for Christians today no longer abstract, far-off things; rather, they challenge Christians' identity and mission in an altogether immediate way.

Also because of this, recent years have seen developments in the debate about the "theology of religions": here the fundamental question concerns the unique significance of Christ in the order of salvation. Do other religions provide ways equivalent to Christianity by which to gain access to the mystery and saving experience of God? If so, why should one engage in proclaiming the gospel to all peoples? If not, what meaning and authenticity can interreligious dialogue have, and what exchange of spiritual goods is truly possible between these different religious experiences?

The theological research that has developed around these questions has tended to move between two extremes: on the one hand, *exclusivism*, holding that no religion besides Christianity can offer salvation (Karl Barth is the twentieth century's most outstanding exponent of this position); on the other, relativistic *pluralism*, holding that Christianity is not the only absolute religion, because God has various names, and does not make himself available only in Jesus Christ (this is the thesis, for example, of the Presbyterian John Hick).

In positive terms, the pluralistic position affirms that non-Christian religions are not only substitutes, but different human responses to the one divine Mystery, understood according to a theocentric, not christocentric, model of salvation. Many of these pluralistic positions recognize Jesus as the Christ, but refuse to accept that the totality of the Word is present in him. The idea of the Christ thus becomes a kind of universal theological-salvific category, of which Christian revelation offers only one example, even if possibly the highest.

An interpretative background for this thesis is offered by the consideration that Asian, and especially Indian, thought is not constructed on the principle of non-contradiction, and thus of opposing positions, but rather of an identity that develops, and can thus express itself in a variety of concrete forms. According to this approach, we are helped to surpass the idea of the uniqueness of the incarnate Word by the very "kenosis" of the divine in Christ, which makes it possible to admit the existence of other ways of historical revelation, analogous to that of the Bible, as for example those in India's religious traditions.

If the exclusivist thesis may today be considered generally abandoned, with the exception of some rather fundamentalist writers and groups, the pluralistic approach is, instead, rejected by the majority, because it deprives historical revelation — and the need for mission — of meaning, rendering vain the value of the unique mediation of Jesus Christ, and of the church as the sacrament of salvation.

We are thus left with the search for an interpretation of the relationship between Christianity and the other world religions in terms of *inclusivism:* holding firm to the necessity of Christ and his mediation, the universal possibility of salvation is nevertheless taken seriously. Various theological tendencies take this approach as their starting point: for some, Christianity fulfills the positive values of the other religions, which are signs of expectation more than salvific mediations (see the positions of Jean Daniélou, Henri de Lubac, and Hans Urs von Balthasar); others recognize a certain sacramentality in the other religions (Yves Congar and Edward Schillebeeckx); for others, finally, the decisive distinction is between history in general and the special history of salvation, on the basis of which the religions have the value of a mediation of transcendence, which is nevertheless only fully achieved in Christianity (this is Karl Rahner's thesis).

As a fruit of the transformation brought about in Christian theology

by the practice of dialogue with the great world religions, theological reflection concerning them appears to be an area of research that is still
open, and not a little problematic, also because of the consequences it
implies for the relationship between the proclamation of the message
and dialogue with cultural and spiritual worlds different from Christianity. Certainly, the Christian faith stands or falls on the recognition that the
fullness of God's self-communication has been realized in the incarnate
Word, who alone is in person "the way, the truth, and the life" (John
14:6), in whom God has reconciled all things to himself.

The confession of the uniqueness of Jesus Christ does not exclude,
however, the recognition of the permanent transcendence of the divine
Mystery, which — while communicating itself in historical form in Trinitarian revelation — remains "absolute," and so free to dispose of itself according to other, possible "economies" of self-communication, no matter how partial these may be. In this sense, the great religions are not
only expressions of the self-transcendence of the human person towards
the holy Mystery, but also possible places of the self-communication of
the loving father-mother of all.

It is the encyclical *Redemptoris Missio* which affirms that for those who
"do not have an opportunity to come to know or accept the gospel revelation or to enter the Church," because they live in "social and cultural
conditions . . . (that) do not permit this, and frequently . . . have been
brought up in other religious traditions," the salvation of Christ "is ac-
cessible by virtue of a grace which, while having a mysterious relationship to the Church, does not make them formally part of the Church but
enlightens them in a way which is accommodated to their spiritual and
material situation. This grace comes from Christ; it is the result of his
sacrifice and is communicated by the Holy Spirit. It enables each person
to attain salvation through his or her free co-operation."[16] The encyclical
makes clear that "the Spirit's presence and activity affect not only individuals but also society and history, peoples, cultures and religions. . . . It is
the Spirit who sows the 'seeds of the Word,' present in various customs
and cultures, preparing them for full maturity in Christ."[17]

In the light of all this, it may be held that the non-Christian religions
contain authentic elements of God's self-communication. For Christ's

16. John Paul II, Encyclical Letter *Redemptoris Missio* (January 25, 1991), no. 10.
17. *Redemptoris Missio*, p. 28.

disciples, however, the only criterion for assessing this can be the revelation achieved in him. If the kingdom of God is also present beyond the visible confines of the church — which is the "universal sacrament" of the Kingdom — the other religions can possess a salvific value, which Christians will recognize in obedience to their faith in the good news of God's love for all his creatures.

This approach implies an attitude of attention and respect towards the different world religions, but does not justify any unwarranted confusion between the fullness of divine revelation achieved in Christ, and whatever light may be available in the other religious traditions and in their sacred texts, through the power of the one, universal, salvific plan of the Father, of the unique and unrepeatable mediation of Christ, and of the action of the Spirit, at work beyond the visible confines of the community of salvation, which is the church.

It is indeed only the affirmation of the uniqueness of the biblical revelation that offers Jesus' disciples the criterion by which to perceive what is true, good, and beautiful — wherever this is present — as well as the authentic ways of salvation contained in the different religions. Reflection on what is the "essence of Christianity" thus becomes necessary for Christians so as to do interreligious dialogue in a way that is at once free from any confusion or abandonment of the truth of the gospel, as well as sincerely open to other religions and to the riches potentially poured out on them by the Spirit of the Risen One.

The Essence of Christianity

For the Christian faith it is Jesus' cry at the ninth hour — perceived in the light of Easter's joyful message — that pierces through the barriers raised by a world without God, and allows the ultimate One to break through into time. Christ, crucified and risen, is the place where the Totally Other came for us, to say who he is — but also to be silent about himself. This is why the encounter with the word of the cross frees and transforms the human heart and human life.

Standing before Pilate, the divine prisoner witnesses to the truth, but not a truth flaunting itself like a logical system, or a fortress of finely honed words. Here truth is the innocent One himself, who — once raised to life again by the Father — comes to meet us in all the discretion of a loving presence; not as something we can possess, but as someone who takes hold of us in the communion of his faithful people.

To be able to recognize the face of this Other, who alone can assuage our aching, hoping hearts, we have to ask — today as ever — what characteristics of Christ we must rediscover and witness to, so as to be able to speak credibly of him to this time without hope, ailing from its lack of passion for the truth. What, in other words, is the horizon opened up by Christian faith to give an account of the hope that is Christ? And this in the contemporary context, where it can seem that human beings have given up looking for any all-encompassing meaning, while at the same time there is a new longing for this very meaning and a new interest in dialogue with the great world religions.

We need to take as our starting point the threefold exodus that characterizes the life of the Word made flesh: exodus from the Father ("exitus a Deo"); from self ("exitus a se"); and towards the Father ("reditus ad Deum"). It is this threefold exodus that allows us to break out of the closed circle of ideological reason and nihilistic pessimism, and out of the prison of a world without God; and it is in the light of this exodus that we can grasp in all its depth the revelation that Jesus offers of the Father and the Consoler-Spirit, and thus the good news about God the Trinity, this eternal story of love, offered also to the other religions as the full self-communication of God's life.

The Exodus of Jesus from the Father

The Word Comes from Silence

"The Word became flesh and lived among us" (John 1:14): according to the Christian faith, Jesus is the Word who comes from silence, the one in whom God comes from his very self out of love for us, the eternal Son made flesh, who opens the way for us into the abyss of the mystery of the divine Trinity. Indeed, the God proclaimed throughout the Bible is a God who leaves himself, a God who has always had time for humankind and who, coming into history, has established a covenant with humanity, opening the way for his people towards the promised Kingdom, which surpasses anything so far achieved.

He is the God who, while communicating himself in the words and deeds of salvation-history, always still eludes human grasp. His advent is thus "re-velation": a lifting of the veil, certainly, but one that yet conceals; a coming, which points the way beyond; at once a self-manifestation and a withdrawal that exerts a powerful attraction.

This interplay of manifestation and concealment attains its highest expression in God's personal self-communication in the incarnate Son: the Word — who says who he is in words — always points us towards the depths of silence from whom he came. God in human flesh is at once both revealed and hidden, "revelatus in absconditate et absconditus in revelatione." The very word "revelatio" (analogously with the Greek "apokàlupsis") refers to this interplay: the prefix "re-" indicates both simple repetition, as well as transformation to an opposite condition. When God comes to reveal himself, he removes the veil that conceals, but also hides himself even more; he communicates himself, but also "veils" himself afresh. . . .

It may thus be said that the Judeo-Christian tradition includes — together with a theology of the Word, and indeed inseparable from it — a theology of Silence: God never speaks except out of an even deeper silence. Silence is not only the fruitful womb from which he comes, but also the place of ultimate fulfillment, where "God will be all in all" (I Cor. 15:28), and all his creatures will be finally and fully themselves in him. In our own silence we yearn for this homeland: this silent God is the world's vocation, the goal of that longing engraved in our very being as creatures.

From silence to silence: this somehow expresses the divine plan, which draws together our beginning and end as creatures, as we strain forward towards the One from whom we come. The mystery of God is that silent place where all things have had their dwelling since the world's first morning; it is the womb from which we issue, in which we move and have our being, the countenance and embrace towards which we journey. Against the backdrop of this divine silence, the Word who comes in the flesh offers himself as light in the darkness, revelation of the eternal love which expresses itself in self-giving till the end, the Son who makes us sons and daughters, and opens the way for us to the mystery of the Father, who is original silence and our last home.

In that "meantime" between the first and last silence, the Word comes, co-eternal in eternity, even if generated and temporally determined by human history. Precisely, however, because "inscribed" in silence, the Word mediates that silence. He is the One who points us back to those silent depths, which are the source and future of his coming, both in time and eternity.

Thus it is that the Word made flesh can only be truly welcomed by a person who listens to this silence, from which the Word comes and towards which he opens the way. Truly to "listen" to the Word is to hear the silence beyond him, the Father whom the Son reveals through the mystery of his unconditional obedience: "Whoever believes in me believes not in me but in him who sent me" (John 12:44). The incarnate Word invites us to go beyond himself, not in the sense that he may be set aside or placed between brackets — that would only close off any access for us to the depths of the divine — but in the sense that the Word is truth and life precisely inasmuch as he is the way (cf. John 14:6), the threshold that opens out onto eternal mystery.

The obedience of faith, therefore, is nothing other than the keenest of listening ("oboedentia" from "ob-audire") to what lies beneath and beyond (ob-) the word immediately heard. The word is truly received only when "transcended," when, that is, it is "obeyed"; when we listen to what lies beyond, behind, and beneath it. To this interplay of manifestation and concealment, present in the very structure of "revelation," there thus corresponds the movement of transcendence proper to the obedience of faith, which does not halt at the immediacy of the Word but goes beyond what is spoken. This is why to receive the Word is a dynamic process, achieved only in a continual "going beyond." Listening like this to that limitless silence, from whom the Word proceeds, in whom he rests and to whom he points, is what fires our tireless search, when, traveling by way of the Word, we reach beyond him.

It is along this path that the Spirit guides believers towards the whole truth (John 16:13), rendering present the memory of Jesus and teaching all things. It is as if the "ecstatic" love of God, by which he comes from silence, and speaks himself in the Word of creation and redemption, calls forth an answering love, equally "ecstatic," which needs to pass beyond the confines of its own world, to walk the boundless paths of silence, towards which revelation faithfully points.

To the exodus from self of the divine silence there thus corresponds — in the unequal relationship between creatures and their Creator — the silent exodus from self of all beings, by which they open themselves to the mystery offered in the Word, in amazement and wonder at the presence of a God who reveals himself in hiddenness and hides himself in revelation. Thus it is that to listen to silence in the Word who comes is to abide in the holy place of adoration, letting oneself be loved by the revealed and hidden God, attracted to him through the unique and necessary mediation of the Son: "No one can come to me unless drawn by the Father who sent me" (John 6:44).

So we come to understand how silence, in which there lives and speaks in us the Word who became flesh in the womb of the Virgin Mother, is the overshadowing of the Spirit, the "ecstasy of God," his living "memory" (John 14:26), the permanent actualization of the Word. The Word thus stands between two silences, Silence of the origins and Silence of the goal, the Father and the Holy Spirit. Between these two silences — the "altissima silentia Dei" — the Word has his home, his splendor, his kenosis. The God who comes is Trinitarian in his deepest mystery, and in the way he communicates himself to human beings.

The Interplay between Revelation and
Listening to the Totally Other

This Trinitarian structure of revelation was long forgotten: especially in modern times, scarred by the claims of the most presumptuous rationalism, God was understood to communicate himself from within a logic of total manifestation, of the pure and simple coming into the open of that which was hidden, expressed by the German term used to translate "revelatio": "Offenbarung" (etymologically: "gestation and opening up of the open"). Thus, the coming of God could be understood as an exhibition with nothing held back: pronouncing itself, absolute mystery consigns itself entirely to the world's grasp; the Eternal One's advent in time thus makes history the "curriculum vitae Dei," God's journeying to become himself.

This was the conviction of Georg Wilhelm Friedrich Hegel: for him, the Christian religion was nothing other than the religion of "Offenbarung," in which is shown forth what God is, so that he may be perceived as he is, not partially as in other religions, but rather in the evident manifestation of his essence.[1] According to this Hegelian understanding, Christianity thus becomes the complete communication of the Absolute in history, the total self-unveiling of the Eternal in time. "Revelatio" is fully achieved in "offenbarung": once the veil is removed, the idea can embrace the divine, and knowledge can fully receive the living God as he manifests himself.

In the beginning, though, it was not thus: to understand revelation as such an unconditioned manifestation is to betray the Judeo-Christian faith in its original and foundational meaning. The Bible, observes André Neher, witnesses to the clash of two different theological mindsets: "The one, settled in the comfortable expectation of a finale that will reconcile all things, places on the other shore — facing the Alpha on this — an Omega, as solidly anchored to terra firma as the symmetrical arches of a suspension bridge. . . . The other, which introduces into this all too beautiful construction a note of uncertainty, does not protect the bridge

---

1. Cf. G. W. F. Hegel, *Vorlesungen über die Philosophie der Religion*, hrsg. V. G. Lasson, 2 Bände (1925; Hamburg, 1974), II, Halbband 2, 32.

against every accidental blow, and does not guarantee the person who crosses it against every risk, *even should such a risk prove to be fatal. . . ."*[2]

While the "suspension-bridge-God" is one who reassures by his word, the "God of the broken arch" restores to human beings the dignity of risk, calling them to accept responsibility for the future without any guarantees, rendering them attentive through silence to the value of the work they accomplish, independently of any result or promised reward.

"God has withdrawn into silence, not *to avoid* human beings, but, on the contrary, *to encounter* them; yet this is all the same an encounter of Silence with silence. . . . Ceasing to be a hiding place, silence becomes the place of the ultimate aggression. Freedom invites God and man to the rendezvous they cannot avoid, but it is the opaque rendezvous of silence."[3] In God's silence the creature's difficult freedom is given full play.

The supreme moment of this "revelation of silence" is the distressing silence that follows Jesus' cry at the ninth hour: Christ crucified is the Word who has come from silence and who dies abandoned, in the silence of the Father. And yet, it is precisely in this abandonment that the greatest love is revealed: in his death on the cross the Son makes his own the silence of death so as to carry this with him into the victory of Easter. The death of the Word opens the way for the eternal Word of life, that death of death itself which is the resurrection of the abandoned Word.

We must, then, approach this center, this heart of revelation with the discretion of those who listen to silence and let the Word speak: this means freeing ourselves from the serious misunderstanding about revelation produced by modern ideology. Teacher of our desires, the God of revelation is he who, in the very act of self-giving, also conceals himself from our gaze, drawing us towards his silent and peaceful depths. Revealed and yet hidden, the God who comes is the God of the promise, of the exodus and of the Kingdom. He is thus revealed not in total vision, but as the Word that opens up paths into the abyss of silence, which is the judgment of every closed ideological claim.

It thus becomes a duty for us never to repeat the Word without first walking long in the paths of silence: "The Father pronounced a Word, who was his Son, and continues to repeat that Word in eternal silence; and

2. A. Neher, *L'esilio della Parola. Dal silenzio biblico al silenzio di Auschwitz* (Casale Monferrato: Marietti, 1983), p. 146.

3. Neher, *L'esilio della Parola,* p. 178.

so the Word must be listened to in the silence of the soul."[4] The God who comes is not a God with ready answers to every question, nor yet a God of cheap certainties, but a demanding God, who, while loving us and giving himself, hides himself, and calls us out of ourselves, on a pilgrimage without return into the depths of his silence, our beginning and our end.

This exodus, this going out of ourselves, is Christian prayer: as the Son lived his coming from the Father in the continuous, adoring attention of his prayer, till the supreme moment of self-giving in Gethsemane, so in following him the disciple will listen to silence, from which the Word comes forth and towards which he invites. Our encounter with Christ in the obedience of faith is nourished by listening and by prayer: and this listening — immersed in the depths of the mystery so as to lead all who live it to be hidden with Christ in God (cf. Col. 3:3) — means to recognize God as the mystery of the world, the adorable womb in whom all things find life, that total otherness to which all must be referred.

To adore, contemplate, and love: this is what is specific to the faith of those who recognize Jesus as the eternal Word come forth from silence, the One who leads human beings to the fresh pastures of life, in the eternal, life-giving silence of the origin and home of all things. From this attentiveness is born faith's questioning of every earthly absolute and hence of every ideological vision. If Christianity is the religion of revelation and of the obedience of faith, it cannot be bartered for any ideology, or sold off to buttress one or other of the various powers at play in history. Faith in the revelation of Jesus, the eternal Word who has come in the flesh, nourishes a permanently critical vigilance that relativizes all human words, measuring them against the one Word which comes forth from silence and is the door to silence. . . .

Jesus' Exodus from Himself

Jesus' Story as a Story of Freedom

"Having loved his own who were in the world, he loved them to the end" (John 13:1): coming from the Father out of love for humanity, Jesus lives

4. S. Giovanni della Croce, *Sentenze. Spunti d'amore*, no. 21, in *Opere*, 2nd ed. (Roma, 1967), p. 1095.

his *exodus from self* till its supreme fulfillment, his death on the cross. This is the journey of his freedom: ready to live for God and humankind, the Nazarene is free from himself in an unconditional way, free to love till the end. The life of the Son in the flesh is an existence entirely received and given.

Jesus is the truly free person, who out of love lives the exodus from self without return, and pays the supreme price. He is well aware that death, mysterious and bitter, awaits him: the story of his faith and hope, his life of prayer, his path strewn with tests of his freedom are the constant proof of this. In the depths of his spirit, darkness and temptation clash with his unconditional dedication to the Father, until he utters the "yes" that brings him to death on the cross.

It is no accident that the public life of this prophet from Galilee begins and ends with two great agonies of freedom: the agony of temptation, and the agony in the garden of Gethsemane. What are these decisive moments, if not the times when he faces the radical alternative and exercises the supreme choice of freedom? Christ makes a radical choice for God, free from himself, free to live for others in an exodus from self without return, to the supreme obedience of the cross: "In the days of his flesh, Jesus offered up prayers and supplications, with loud cries and tears, to the one who was able to save him from death, and he was heard because of his reverent submission. Although he was a Son, he learned obedience through what he suffered . . ." (Heb. 5:7-8).

The bareness of the account of Jesus' temptation in Mark (1:12-13), the more developed presentation of three temptations in Matthew and Luke (Matt. 4:1-11; Luke 4:1-13), all show how the early Christian community understood that this episode represented a decisive turning point in the history of salvation: the fullness of times had come! Just as Israel in the desert was really tested, so Jesus is truly tempted: the context is the same, the desert of aloneness with God; the indications of time are charged with theological significance — the forty days, which bring to mind the forty years of the Exodus and the time spent by Moses on the mountain (cf. Exod. 24:18 and 34:28); there are three trials, corresponding to those experienced by the chosen people during their journey towards the Promised Land.

While, however, Israel succumbs, Jesus triumphs. The basic temptation is the same: to resist God's plan of salvation, to give in to the supreme lie, which seduced the first Adam, trusting in oneself and the power of the world rather than in God and his "weakness." It is the alternative offered by Augustine: "Love of self till God is forgotten, or love of God till self is forgotten."[5]

Jesus experiences the temptation's seductive pull, the apparently superior effectiveness it promises. He stands on the very brink: on the one hand, he knows the fascination of the political messianism of his time, encountered among his people as he shared their suffering under oppression; on the other, there rises before him the messianism of prophetic obedience, which he had come to know in his conversations with his Father, and especially through reading the scriptures about the suffering servant and the prophets.

The Nazarene says "no" to the temptations of his time: he does not seek easy consensus or pander to people's expectations, but rather subverts them. Jesus chooses the Father: with an act of sovereign freedom he prefers obedience to God and abnegation of self to obedience to self, which implies the rejection of God. He does not succumb under the weight of the apparently obvious, or to the pull of immediate success: he believes in the Father with indestructible confidence, and means to carry out that Father's plan, no matter how mysterious and painful it may seem. In the hour of temptation, Jesus reaffirms his freedom from himself, free for the Father and for others, free with the freedom of love: in him, the unconditionally obedient servant, the stairway of prophetic obedience reaches its summit. Considered mad by his own ("He has gone out of his mind": Mark 3:21), accused by the scribes of being possessed (cf. Mark 3:22 and parallels), dismissed as an impostor by the powerful (cf. Matt. 27:63), he feels the whole weight of the hostility accumulating against him. He is not saddened by the accusations, but by the hardness of heart from which they issue (cf. Mark 3:5).

Why the powerful are hostile to the Nazarene is readily understood: his unheard-of claims irritate them, and his popularity frightens them. By his words and life, Jesus undermines their certainties, and, with his success among the people, threatens to shake the precarious status quo to its very foundations, founded as it is on compromise between the Roman occupiers and the country's comfortable classes. Jesus, though, is too free to draw back before their threats: and so he continues along his road, faithful to the radical "yes" he has said to the Father. He becomes, it is

---

5. St. Augustine, *De Civitate Dei* 14.28; PL 41:456.

true, more careful, managing to flee from attempts to stone and arrest him; he avoids confrontation. But, in this crucible of suffering, he also brings into sharper focus the choice that will mark the turning point in his work: the decisive journey to Jerusalem, fulfillment of his vocation. "The city of the great King" (Matt. 5:35) is the place where the destinies of Israel and of her prophets must be fulfilled (cf. Luke 13:33). Jesus foresees what awaits him there as a consequence of the choice expressed in his life and message: the rejection he met with in Galilee, much deeper than the easy enthusiasm of the crowds, has left no room for doubt that he will have to drink to the lees the chalice prepared for the just, bringing to completion the supreme offering of his life. In this sense, it is the "crisis" pervading the whole "Galilean spring" that brings him to Jerusalem: a painful experience of finitude, accepted in self-giving to the Father and with faith in the final victory of justice and of love.

With the entry into Jerusalem the story of the passion begins in earnest. Jesus heads there with determination (cf. Luke 9:51: literally "he set his face like flint towards Jerusalem"), walking ahead of his own, who follow him disconcerted. In David's city, the conflict reaches its apex: the Sanhedrin is deeply involved now, as are both the lay and priestly aristocracies that body represents. The Nazarene is aware of the mystery of iniquity which is about to play itself out in his regard, but he confronts it with the strength of one who sees in a death unjustly inflicted his own free self-giving, lived in obedience to the Father, a death which therefore brings life. Accounts of the last supper are proof of this, when the servant entrusts to his own the memorial of the new covenant in his blood.

Only a little later, Jesus will find himself alone in the garden of Gethsemane: it is the moment when he is faced with the final consequence of his choice. He experiences — to the point of sweating blood (cf. Luke 22:24) — the temptation of drawing back from paying the painful price of his love. The evangelists speak of his anguish, his sadness, his fear. He feels an immense need for the company of his friends: "Remain here; and stay awake with me" (Matt. 26:38). But he is left to face his future alone, as happens to all of us when we are called to make life's fundamental choices: "Could you not stay awake with me one hour?" (Matt. 26:40). Yet again, he is faced, in the most violent of ways, with the radical alternative: to save his own life or lose it, to choose between his own will and the Father's: "Abba, Father, for you all things are possible; remove this cup from me" (Mark 14:36 and parallels). At the moment when he confirms the "yes" of his radical freedom, he clings totally to the Father and calls to him with the name of trust and tenderness: "Abba . . . yet, not what I want, but what you want." The "yes" of Jesus is born of unconditional love: his freedom is the freedom of love! At the supreme moment, he chooses once again to give himself, he places himself in the Father's hands with limitless trust, he lives his freedom as liberation, freedom from self, freedom for the Father and others. It is the freedom of one who finds his life by losing it (cf. Mark 8:35), able to risk everything for love; it is the daring of one who gives all.

Unconditionally free, Jesus lives out the exodus from self for the Father and others, till the final loneliness of abandonment on the cross: this is his fundamental option, which makes him truly the "free person," and transforms the death he unjustly undergoes into a free self-giving, lived in obedience to the Father, and consequently life-giving. This is the context of Jesus' trial: it is the hour of his enemies, "the power of darkness" (Luke 22:53). In the eyes of the Sanhedrin he is the blasphemer (cf. Mark 14:53-65 and parallels), who with his words and deeds (above all the "scandalous" cleansing of the temple: cf. Mark 11:15-18 and parallels) has merited death according to the Law (cf. Deut. 17:12). And yet Jesus was not subjected to the punishment reserved for blasphemers, which was stoning (cf. Lev. 24:14); he was punished by the Roman occupiers, receiving the sentence inflicted on slaves who deserted, and on those who subverted the empire, the ignominious death on the cross. His sentence was, in the end, a political one, as is witnessed by the "titulus crucis," the inscription with the cause of his condemnation, placed on the wood of shame: "Jesus of Nazareth, the King of the Jews" (John 19:19). His death could be considered a judicial murder, with political and religious significance: Good Friday (April 7th of the year 30?) is for the Law the day when the blasphemer dies, and for the powerful, the day of the death of one who sought to subvert the status quo. Christian faith recognizes in it, instead, the day of the death of the Son of the immortal God, out of love of us.

The Cross as the Story of the Trinity

According to the New Testament, Good Friday sees a series of dramatic events in each of which Jesus is "handed over." The first of these is his betrayal by Judas, when Jesus' friend consigns him to his enemies: "Then Judas Iscariot, who was one of the twelve, went to the chief priests in order to betray him to them" (Mark 14:10). In its turn the Sanhedrin, guardian and representative of the Law, hands the blasphemer over to Caesar's representative: "As soon as it was morning, the chief priests held a consultation with the elders and scribes and the whole council. They bound Jesus, led him away, and handed him over to Pilate" (Mark 15:1). Pilate, while convinced of the prisoner's innocence — "What evil has he done?" (Mark 15:14) — yields to the pressure of the mob incited by the leaders (cf. 15:11): "After flogging Jesus, he handed him over to be crucified" (Mark 15:15).

Abandoned by all, Jesus is alone in living his exodus from himself till the last. If this were the end, though, his death would be just one more of history's unjust executions, with an innocent person crying out in the face of the world's injustice. The early Christian community — transformed by the Easter experience — knows, instead, that this is *not* the case: that is why this community recounts three other, mysterious ways in which Jesus is handed over.

The first is when the Son hands over his own self. Paul puts it clearly: "The life I live now in the flesh I live by faith in the Son of God, who loved me and gave himself for me" (Gal. 2:20). The Son hands himself over to his God and Father for love of us: handing himself over like this, the Crucified One takes upon himself the burden of the world's past, present, and future suffering and sin; he journeys to the frontiers of furthest exile from God, so as to make his own the exile of sinners, in the self-offering and reconciliation of Easter. "Christ redeemed us from the curse of the law by becoming a curse for us — for it is written, 'Cursed is everyone who hangs on a tree' — in order that in Christ Jesus the blessing of Abraham might come to the Gentiles, so that we might receive the promise of the Spirit through faith" (Gal. 3:13-14). The cry of the dying Jesus expresses the extreme of suffering and exile that the Son desired to make his own, so as to journey to the furthest outposts of the world's sorrow, and lead this sorrow to reconciliation with the Father: "My God, my God, why have you forsaken me?" (Mark 15:34; cf. Matt. 27:46).

To the fact that the Son handed himself over corresponds the fact that the Father too handed him over: "The Son of Man is to be betrayed into human hands and they will kill him" (Mark 9:31 and parallels). It is not merely human beings, into whose hands Jesus is consigned, that hand him over, and neither is it he alone who does this, since the verb here is in the passive. It will be God, his Father, who will hand him over, he "who did not withhold his own Son, but gave him up for all of us" (Rom. 8:32). It is in the Father's giving up of his own Son for us in this way that he manifests the depths of his love: "In this is love, not that we loved God but that he loved us and sent his Son to be the atoning sacrifice for our sins" (1 John 4:10).

Thus it is that at the cross the Father too makes history: giving up his own Son, he pronounces judgment on the gravity of the world's sin, but also shows the greatness of his merciful love for us. The cross reveals that "God (the Father) is love" (1 John 4:8-16!). The suffering of the Father — who does not spare his own Son but gives him up for us all (cf. Rom. 8:32) — was already signified in Abraham's sacrifice of his "only-begotten" son, Isaac (cf. Gen. 22:2). This is simply the other name of his love: for the Son, as for the Father, the supreme, sorrowful giving up is the sign of that love which comes from above and changes history: "No one has greater love than this, to lay down one's life for one's friends. . . . I have called you friends, because I have made known to you everything that I have heard from my Father" (John 15:13, 15).

To the suffering of the Son, "who loved me and gave himself up for me" (Gal. 2:20), there thus corresponds the silent suffering of the Father: God suffers on the cross as Father, who offers — as well as in the Son — his very self to death for us. The cross is the story of God's love for the world: a love that does not simply bear suffering, but chooses it. While the Greeks and Romans could only conceive of suffering imposed, borne passively, and consequently imperfect, suffering that thus calls for a theory of divine impassibility, the Christian God reveals a suffering that is active, freely chosen, and perfect with the perfection of love: this is not a God outside the world's pain, a passive spectator in unalterable perfection. The living God makes his own and lives the suffering of his creatures in the most intense way, in a suffering that is active, a gift and self-offering from which there flows new life for the world. Ever since that first Good Friday we know that the story of human suffering is also the story of the Christian God: he is present in that story, suffering with human beings and sharing with them the immense value of suffering offered for love. This is the God who gives meaning to the world's suffering, because he took it upon himself to the point of making it his own, love-filled suffering.

Story of the Son, story of the Father, the cross is no less the story of the Spirit: the supreme act of self-giving is the sacrificial offering of the Spirit, as John the evangelist perceived: "Then he bowed his head and gave up his spirit" (John 19:30). It is "with an eternal Spirit" that the Christ "offered himself without stain to God" (Heb. 9:14). On the cross, the Crucified One gives up to the Father the very Spirit the Father had first given him, the Spirit he will receive again on the day of the resurrection. Good Friday, when the Son hands himself over to the Father, and when the Father gives the Son up to death for sinners, is also the day when the Spirit is handed over by the Son to the Father, so that the Son may be abandoned, far from God, in the company of sinners. This is the hour of death *in* God, of the Father's abandonment of the Son in their yet deeper communion of love, fully achieved in the handing over of the Spirit to the Father, which makes possible the supreme exodus of the Son into the otherness of the world, his becoming a "curse" in the land of those cursed by God, so that they together with him may enter into the glory of Easter reconciliation.

Without this handing over of the Spirit, the cross would not manifest its full depths as a saving and Trinitarian event: if the Spirit had not let himself be handed over in the silence of death, with all the abandonment that this entailed, the hour of darkness could be misunderstood as the dark death of God, the incomprehensible withering away of the Absolute, and would not be understood for what it really is, an act which happens in God, an event in the history of the love of the immortal God, for whom the Son enters into starkest otherness from his Father in obedience to him, to reach the place where he can encounter sinners. "For our sake he made him to be sin who knew no sin so that in him we might become the righteousness of God" (2 Cor. 5:21).

On the cross the Spirit too makes history: history in God, because — handed over to the Father — he renders possible the otherness of the Son from the Father, in solidarity with sinners, even though always in the infinite communion expressed in the sacrificial obedience of the Crucified One. Yet the Spirit makes history for us, too, because on the cross he makes the Son close to us, allowing those who are far off to walk an open road with the Son from exile back to the home of Trinitarian communion. Story of the Son, of the Father, and of the Spirit, the cross is the Trinitarian story of God: the Trinity takes to itself the exile of the world subjected to sin, in order that this exile may enter at Easter into the home of Trinitarian communion. The cross is our story, because it is the Trinitarian story of God: it does not proclaim the blasphemy of a death *of* God to make room for human beings imprisoned in their self-sufficiency; it proclaims, rather, the good news of death *in* God, so that human beings may live with the life of the immortal God, sharing in Trinitarian communion, in a way made possible thanks to that death.

On the cross "home" goes into exile, so that exile may go "home": this is the key to history! The cross thus points to Easter: the hour of separation points to the hour of reconciliation, the empire of death to the triumph of life! The otherness of the Son from the Father on Good Friday, wrought in the painful handing over of the Spirit, the exodus from self till the supreme abandonment on the cross, his "descent into hell" in solidarity with all those who were, are, and will be prisoners of sin and of death, all these are directed, in the unity of the paschal mystery, to the reconciliation of the Son with the Father, achieved on the "third day."

Jesus' Exodus to the Father

Experiencing Easter

"If Christ has not been raised, then our proclamation has been in vain and your faith has been in vain" (1 Cor. 15:14): it is the resurrection which reveals Jesus in his fullness as *the Christ, Lord of life,* the Son in the flesh who lives the exodus from this world to the Father, and then returns to the glory from which he came ("reditus ad Deum"). The Risen One witnesses to the victorious otherness of God with respect to this world; to the Ultimate One with respect to all that is penultimate, revealed as such precisely in the judgment pronounced in the cross and resurrection. Upon the painful separation of the abandonment on the cross, there follows the communion of the resurrection: the death in God for the world on Good Friday leads into Easter and the life of the world in God; the exodus from self of the Son till death is transformed into the exodus of the Son towards the Father, and of the world together with him. Precisely because Jesus' death is a death in love, it is also the death of death, a death which does not divide but rather reconciles, which does not deny the oneness of God but supremely affirms it, both in itself and for the world. If on the cross the Son gives himself up to the Father, thus entering into the abyss of abandonment by God, in the resurrection the Father gives the Spirit to the Son, taking up the world with him and in him into infinite divine communion: one is the Triune God who acts on the cross and in the resurrection, one is the Trinitarian story of God, one is the plan of salvation that is achieved in these two moments.

How did the disciples come to recognize the exodus of Jesus towards his Father? In the beginning there was the experience of an encounter: to those who fled on Good Friday Jesus showed himself alive (cf. Acts 1:3). This encounter was so decisive for them that their existence was totally transformed: fear was replaced by courage; flight by mission. Those who had fled became witnesses, and remained so until death, in a life given unconditionally to the One they had betrayed in the "hour of darkness."

What had happened? There is a hiatus between sunset on Good Friday and the dawn of Easter, an interruption in which happened something so important as to give birth to the Christian movement in history. Where the "lay" historian can only note this "new beginning" — unable to explain its causes after the failure of the various "liberal" interpretations of the Easter faith which tended to suggest that this was a purely subjective experience of the disciples — Christian proclamation, as recorded in the New Testament, confesses the encounter with the Risen One as an experience of grace; and it gives us access to this experience especially through the accounts of the apparitions.[6]

These accounts cannot be harmonized among themselves in terms of time and place: they are, however, all constructed on the same pattern, allowing us to grasp the fundamental elements of the experience to which they testify. There is always the initiative of the Risen One, the process of recognition on the part of the disciples, and then mission, which makes them witnesses of what they "heard and saw with their own eyes and contemplated and touched with their own hands" (cf. 1 John 1:1). The initiative of the Risen One, the fact, that is, that it is he who shows himself alive (cf. Acts 1:3), who "appears,"[7] indicates that the experience of these first Christians had an "objective" character: it was

6. Cf. the Pauline tradition: 1 Cor. 15:5-8; the Marcan tradition: Mark 16:9-20; the Matthean tradition: Matt. 28:9-10, 16-20; the Lucan tradition: Luke 24:13-53; and the Johannine: John 20:14-29 and chap. 21.

7. Cf. the verb ōphthē, used in 1 Cor. 15:3-8 and Luke 24:34. In the Greek translation of the Old Testament (the Septuagint) the word is used to describe the divine manifestations, the theophanies: cf. Gen. 12:7; 17:1; 18:1; 26:2.

something that "came" towards them, not simply something that "came to be" within them. It was not emotions of faith and love that created their object, but the Living One who stirred up that faith and love in a new way.

This does not exclude, however, a process of spiritual growth, necessary so that the first believers might open themselves from within to what had happened in Jesus; a witness to this is the gradual journey — carefully underlined by the New Testament — which leads the disciples from amazement and doubt to recognition of the Risen One: "Then their eyes were opened and they recognized him" (Luke 24:31). This process points to the subjective and spiritual dimension of the foundational experience of the Christian faith, and grounds the freedom of faith's "yes."

This, then, is how the experience of the encounter happens: in a relationship of direct and risk-laden recognition, the Living One offers himself to his own, and renders them, too, alive with new life, witnesses of the encounter with him which marks their lives forever: "Go into all the world and proclaim the good news to the whole creation" (Mark 16:15). "You killed the author of life, whom God raised from the dead. To this we are witnesses" (Acts 3:15).

The Easter experience — both objective and subjective — is thus presented as an experience of transformation: it is the source of mission; it generates the movement of proclamation that will spread to the very ends of the earth. It is the experience of a double identity in contradiction: the first, between the risen Christ and the One humiliated on the cross; the second, between those who fled on Good Friday and the witnesses of Easter. In the Risen One is recognized the crucified; and this recognition, which binds supreme exaltation to deepest shame, has the effect of transforming the fear of the disciples into courage; they become new persons, able to love the dignity of the new life they have received more than life itself, till the point of martyrdom.

From Faith Narrated to Faith Defined

In fact, the confession of faith expressed in the formulas "Jesus is the Christ" (that is, the messiah, the anointed), "Jesus is the Lord" — which confer on the One who suffered such humiliation the glorious title of

Messiah of divine condition — witnesses to this unheard-of identity in contradiction, experienced when the humble Nazarene was recognized in the Risen One. This confession constitutes the "creed" of the first communities in its most concentrated form, and is also the foundation of the most ancient Christian theology. The events of the life of the historical Jesus, especially as recorded by the Gospels — where historical material and Easter rereading are continuously mixed, without, though, the one supplanting the other — were reconsidered in the light of the proclamation of the death and resurrection of the Nazarene, founded on the experience of the encounter with the Risen One handed on in the accounts of the apparitions.

The Son of man, understood according to the messianic expectation expressed, for example, by the prophet Daniel (cf. 7:13ff.), is the Son of God, professed in the light of Easter. The history of salvation before Christ[8] and the first beginnings of the world[9] are interpreted in an analogous way. The Easter faith also presses forward, towards the contemporary community — as witnessed by the lively portrait of the early church in the Acts of the Apostles — and towards the furthest horizon of hope and expectation — as happens, for example, in the "theology of history" of the Book of Revelation. Paul's mighty theological construction — which inaugurates the Christian scriptures — comes into being precisely when to the risen Lord, encountered on the road to Damascus, he refers the decisive questions of life, death, evil, salvation, law, grace, and the promised future. For the early church as for Israel before her, to confess her Lord means to tell the story of his deeds, and to recognize his work in the whole of history, both of the individual and of the community.[10]

The "credo" of the origins is thus gradually consolidated in formulas, which sum up the essential elements present in the scriptural witness. In reaction to the various reductive approaches that emerge, tending especially to diminish the scandal of the eternal Son being made flesh, attention is progressively focused on the incarnation from the Virgin, in a way that culminates in ever greater attention to the double "birth," the

8. See, for example, the "Bible of Matthew," i.e., the very wide use the first Gospel makes of quotations from the Old Testament to speak of the Son of David, in whom the kingdom of God comes to us.

9. Thus, for example, Col. 1:15 says that creation came about with a view to Christ and through him.

10. Cf. the confession of faith of people of the Old Testament in Deut. 5:1ff.

earthly birth from Mary, and the eternal birth from the Father (cf. the so-called "Apostles' Creed").

In fact, from the earliest times of the Christian movement, there were attempts to eliminate the scandalous identity in contradiction between Jesus the Nazarene and the Lord proclaimed at Easter. Thus, the Docetists and Ebionites, even though moving in opposite directions, started from the same felt need to safeguard the divinity of God: to that end, the former denied the true humanity of Christ — reducing it to an appearance, "doxa," whence "docetists" — while the latter diminished his divine condition, making of him a mere creature — a poor man, "ebion," whence "ebionites." For the former, Jesus was merely an apparition of the divinity, intended to teach humankind the path of saving knowledge ("gnosis"); for the latter, he was no more than a just man adopted by God as Son.

Over against these opposing interpretations, one can understand how the narrative simplicity of the ancient creeds sounded scandalous: if, on the one hand, telling the human story of the Son of God prevented the elimination of one or other of the poles of the Easter contradiction, on the other it underscored the unheard-of identity between the Crucified and Risen One, without emptying the cross of its reality, but also without depriving the resurrection of its newness and power.

The third century brings with it a new development in the tendencies that seek to reduce the complex totality of the Christian mystery. At Rome, first Praxeas, and then Sabellius, develop an interpretation linked to docetism, and known as "modalism." The human story of Jesus is understood here as an epiphany of the divine, or as the "mode" by which the one God appears in the midst of humanity. Monotheism thus appears to be safeguarded, and the problem of the unity of Christ is solved: the result obtained, however, even if it may seem consistent from the logical point of view, empties the paradox of Christian faith of its true meaning.

The same may be said of the position that opposed modalism: the mature "adoptionism" of the third century, which — without denying that Christ is God — affirms that he became such when the Father filled with his Spirit the unique and exemplary man who was the Nazarene. In the fourth century these ideas are connected with Arius, a priest from Egyptian Alexandria: he recognizes in Christ the Son created by the Father at the beginning of the creation of the world to be the mediator and instrument of his work of creation. Inasmuch as a creature, though, he would be essentially different from the Father, and thus able to become, to be incarnated, and to suffer. Placing the Son on the side of creatures, Arius satisfies the demands of middle Platonic thought, but he dissolves the Christian scandal of identity in contradiction between the crucified Nazarene and the Son of God.

It is the fathers of the church in the third and fourth centuries who respond to these different tendencies: their thought flows into the solemn "creed" of the Council of Nicea (325), organized in two sections, of which the first proclaims the pre-existence of the Lord Jesus, his being equal to the Father and his role in creation, while the second takes up the history of the Incarnate, Crucified, and Risen One. Proclaiming the divinity of Jesus, his "consubstantiality" with the Father — that is, his equality in divinity — Nicea distances itself from the hellenization of the Christian faith, represented by the Arian thesis of a created Son, intermediate between God and the world. This Son, "true God from true God," is also the subject of the second section, where the horizontal and historical scheme of the more ancient creeds is again taken. This link underlines the salvific value of the ontological affirmations, even if it greatly modifies the structure of the traditional confession of faith: the narration of the events becomes one plane, linked vertically to the other plane, that of the pre-existence. To the historical-horizontal scheme characteristic of the ancient creeds, there thus succeeds a metaphysical-vertical scheme, which, while still including the narrative section, reduces its weight in favor of a more conceptual and ontological approach.

In the fifth century there emerge the extreme expressions of the two schools that characterized Christian patristic thought, the Alexandrian and the Antiochene. The Antiochene school bears the influence of Aristotelian philosophy and of an exegesis attentive to the letter of the biblical texts: it accentuates the distinction of the divinity from the concrete humanity of the Lord Jesus. Along these lines, Nestorius, patriarch of Constantinople, while still affirming the divinity of Christ, wanted at the same time to take his full, real humanity seriously: he thus proposed a moral unity between the man assumed, Jesus, and the eternal Word, founded on the harmony of will and action.

The Alexandrines, on the contrary, influenced by Platonic philosophy, accentuated the unity of the divine and human in Jesus Christ, but to the point of confusing them. The extreme expression of this tendency is the "monophysitism" of Eutychius, archimandrite of the monks of Constantinople, who so underlined the unity of Christ as to speak of "one nature" in him after the union. To these opposing reductive positions the Council of Chalcedon (451) replies by way of a definition which, even if it has influenced the history of christology more than any other, has never been used in the context of worship, because it altogether lacks the historical-narrative section, still to be found, instead, in the creeds of Nicea and Constantinople.

For the narration of events Chalcedon entirely substitutes the enunciation of Christ's metaphysical structure. Through a movement of successive affirmations and negations it affirms the unity of the divine person of the one and same Christ, and the two natures, divine and human, between which there is neither mixture nor reciprocal transformation (against the monophysite confusion), nor division and separation (against Nestorian dualism). In this way, Chalcedon gathered the results of the christological elaborations of the first centuries, expressing them in the language of Greek thought: this has translated into static, conceptual categories the identity in contradiction expressed in a historical, dynamic manner in the Easter formulas.

It cannot be denied that the Chalcedonian formula bears the marks of a compromise: if, on the one hand, this does not dissolve the Christian paradox, on the other it transposes the paradox into a new and different cultural horizon and language with respect to the New Testament. In this sense, Chalcedon is an example of the inculturation of the Christian faith, even if with a certain weakening of the narrative, existential, and prophetic power of the original message. Jesus' exodus to the Father, however, is perceived in all its significance, and linked to his original exodus from the Father: the faith of the origins, even if expressed in categories unfamiliar to the biblical world, is maintained here in its original scandalous power. The good news of the threefold exodus of Jesus is not lost, and, precisely thanks to the fidelity to the faith expressed at Chalcedon, neither will it be lost in the successive historical development of Christian doctrine.

God, the Father, Is Love

By his threefold exodus, Jesus reveals to us the face of God his Father, rooting himself in the faith of Israel and, at the same time, surpassing

45

that faith beyond every desire and expectation: "God is love. God's love was revealed among us in this way: God sent his only Son into the world so that we might live through him" (1 John 4:8-9).

The Humility of the Living God

It is a Hebrew word that expresses most intensely the special trait of the God of the chosen people, the Father of Israel: it renders God's love with the powerful image of a mother's womb, "rachamim." God is viscerally in love with human beings: besides being a Father full of "hesed," of love faithful and strong, the God of the Bible is also a tender and merciful Father. This is how he is presented in Isaiah 49:14-16: "Zion said, 'The Lord has forsaken me, my Lord has forgotten me.' Can a woman forget her nursing child, or show no compassion for the child of her womb? Even these may forget, yet I will not forget you. See, I have inscribed you on the palms of my hands."

Israel's God is a motherly God, who knows what tenderness is, with his creatures always before his eyes, because they are engraved on the palm of his hand. This God is so maternal that he makes himself little so we may live: this is the Hebrew teaching of "zim-zum," God's "contraction." In this, Hebrew mysticism discerns the very heart of the mystery of creation: God humbles himself, giving his creatures room to live; God creates us free in his sight. He loves us so much that he takes the risk of our freedom, giving us the freedom even to tell him: "I do not know who you are." This is divine humility: the God of the Bible is a humble God, the Father of mercies, the God who makes himself small so that human beings may live.

This God looks for "teshuva" in his creatures, a word usually translated by "conversion," but strictly speaking meaning "return." God yearns for us to return to his house. He has created us free out of love, and, whenever we stray far from him, it is with love that he awaits our return. Here we catch a glimpse of the Father depicted in Jesus' parable of the prodigal son (Luke 15:11ff.), a powerful presentation of how the Bible reveals God as full of tenderness and mercy. Hosea 11:8 moves in the same direction: "How can I give you up, Ephraim? How can I hand you over, O Israel? . . . My heart recoils within me; my compassion grows warm and tender."

This God, who turns towards human beings out of love, who has made himself a father and mother with "entrails of mercy," is the God of the "shekinah," who, that is, "stands ready" in the midst of his people, sharing their sorrows and joys. The Father of Israel is anything but a distant, cold, ideological god who crushes human beings: he is, instead, a God of tenderness even when he judges, because his is a judgment in truth and love, telling us the truth about ourselves, because he searches and knows us as no other can. He is the father-mother God of tenderness and forgiveness, of mercy and humility, who gives us freedom to live and adhere to the covenant, and who calls us untiringly to conversion, to return to his divine heart, to live with the heart of his children.

Jesus called this God "abbà," a title of tenderness with which children were fond of addressing their father, and which even adults used to express trust. Jesus was the first Jew to address God in this way: this is the deeply meaningful invocation we hear him use in Mark 14:32-36, at the hour of his most bitter sorrow, when everything seems to be collapsing, and his loneliness is complete, because even the disciples are not able to stay awake just one hour with him: "Abba, Father, for you all things are possible; remove this cup from me; yet not what I want, but what you want."

This is the Father into whose hands Jesus entrusts his spirit. Jesus' Father is a God able to come out of himself and to suffer for love of his creatures; not only humble, not only a God of compassion and tenderness, but a God so free from himself as to be ready to pay the supreme price of love. As Abraham sacrifices Isaac for love of God, so the Father of Jesus sacrifices the one he loves, the Isaac of the new and eternal covenant, for love of humankind (cf. Gen. 22 and Rom. 8:32). As Origen says: "God competes magnificently in generosity with humankind: Abraham offered God a mortal son without that son dying; God handed over to death the immortal Son for humanity."[11]

Jesus' Father is thus a God capable of suffering out of love: this is the conviction John Paul II expresses in *Dominum et vivificantem* when he speaks of a mystery of suffering hidden in God's heart (cf. nos. 39 and 41). The ancient Councils of the Church said the same: "Deus passus est" — "God suffered." God's suffering is not a sign of weakness or limitation, nor is it passive, accepted only because unavoidable. It is, rather, active,

---

11. Origen, *Homilia in Genesim* 8; SC 123:36-43.

freely accepted out of love for the beloved. Here we are shown the very heart of God: the Father suffers because he loves us, because he created us free, and of his own free will ran the risk of our freedom. He is the God of freedom because he is the God of love, and he is the Father of love because he is free from himself, and wants us to be free in his presence. He is like the Father in the parable, who awaits our return and suffers because we are far from him, and will celebrate when we return. Our sin is not a matter of indifference for his divine heart. God suffers for each one of the sins of his children: if, though, this suffering is active and not passive, if, that is, it is a suffering that God chooses freely out of love, then its other name is "agape," charity. "Deus caritas est": God, the Father, is love (1 John 4:8, 16). Jesus' Father is long-suffering love, joyful, faithful, welcoming love, the hopeful love that awaits our return. . . .

God, Who Is Love

The Father of Jesus is love, both in himself and for the world: beginning with what he accomplished for humanity in creation and redemption, as presented by the fullness of revelation in Christ, God the Father may be contemplated in all the depth of his being as the One who loves in freedom, who has always loved, and will always love, as the God-for-us who sends his Son, God-with-us. "Whoever does not love does not know God, for God is love. God's love was revealed among us in this way: God sent his only Son into the world so that we might live through him. In this is love, not that we loved God but that he loved us and sent his Son to be the atoning sacrifice for our sins. . . . So we have known and believe the love that God has for us. God is love, and those who abide in love abide in God, and God abides in them" (1 John 4:8-10, 16).

Because he loves us, the Father knows everything: "Ubi amor, ibi oculus" (Richard of St. Victor) — nothing is hidden from Love! This is the mystery of divine omniscience, which is not a neutral, detached kind of knowing, but is rather in the biblical sense a knowing, a being intimately acquainted with, a knowing that is loving, attentive, and engaged, as is revealed in the relationship between the Father and the Son, and between Jesus and his own: "I am the good shepherd. I know my own and my own know me, just as the Father knows me and I know the Father. And I lay down my life for the sheep" (John 10:14-15). Thus understood, divine omniscience is not in competition with the freedom of the creature, just as loving knowledge — if the love is true — does not diminish the freedom of the beloved!

It is in this light, too, that God the Father's omnipotence is to be understood: he who is absolute fullness of life can do everything in love! In love he orders all things to good: this is the mystery of his providence! Precisely because his power is infinite in love, and because love is true in freedom, the Father never exercises his power against the freedom of his creatures: rather, he even bears appearing powerless, or deaf to the groans of the dying! He "who desires everyone to be saved and to come to the knowledge of the truth" (1 Tim. 2:4) will not save anyone against their will.

It is here that, to some degree at any rate, light is thrown on his otherwise intolerable tolerance of evil: "Si Deus iustus, unde malum?" — "If God is just, why is there evil?" Precisely because Jesus' Father is a just God, who loves us in freedom, he takes the risk of love, accepts the possibility of rejection, with all the consequences deriving from this for the whole of creation.[12] Evil in the world is the paradoxical sign that divine omnipotence is love in freedom, a capacity for infinite respect and active compassion, to the point of appearing even as weakness: "Divine compassion does not remove creatures from suffering, but it does not abandon them, and assists them till the end, even without showing itself" (Ignatius Silone).

Inasmuch as God is the eternal source and goal of every life, he is beyond space: not because he is spatially beyond, but because he enfolds all things in his embrace, limitlessly standing over all things and remaining in all things. This is the mystery of divine omnipresence, understood as the omnipresence of love: God, the Father, is immense in love! This omnipresence is ordered to the supreme divine presence in history, the personal presence of the incarnate Son: in the Beloved, made flesh for us, the seed of receptivity to love is sown in all creatures, rendering them open to the loving divine omnipresence. Precisely thus, he who is higher than every height of ours can make himself more intimate to us than we are to ourselves: "Those who love me will keep my word, and my Father will love them, and we will come to them and make our home with them" (John 14:23)!

12. Cf. Rom. 8:20, 22.

God as Father is also beyond time: not because he is temporally outside of time, but because he enfolds in himself all becoming, as the eternal beginning and end of all things. This is the mystery of divine eternity, perennial presence of that life which is the source of all life, or, in biblical terms, the daily faithfulness of his love. In this sense, too, divine immutability is to be understood: not as the indifference of a slothful God or the immobility of a dead God, but rather the dynamism of a living God, always the same and always new in love, and thus absolutely faithful to his promises. God does not change, because he always loves, today and forever: God is unchangeable in the fidelity of his love! Precisely thus, in this most free fidelity, he is always new in love!

To this width, height, and depth of the love of God the Father the creature can only respond by celebrating his glory: this is what the Judeo-Christian tradition means by its proclamation of the unity and uniqueness of God. This confession — which unites Israel, Christianity, and Islam — is much more than the profession of an abstract idea: it is an act of adoration and a commitment, a doxology and an engagement: "Hear, O Israel. The Lord is our God, the Lord alone. You shall love the Lord your God with all your heart, and with all your soul, and with all your might" (Deut. 6:4-5).

Confessing this one God means entering the mystery of his unity, and committing oneself to work so that all human beings may also know justice and peace. For the Christian faith, this becomes truly possible only when the divine unity opens itself to us, offering itself as the unity of Love: of Love that loves, of Love that is loved, and of Love that unites God and the world in freedom. It is here that the confession of faith in the Father must find completion in the confession of the Trinity, of the one God as Love, including both distinction and openness to the other so as to take them both into the movement of eternal love. To confess the unity of God means to enter the unity of God: but to enter into this divine unity means to let oneself become involved in the eternal story of love. It is thus that the radicalization of Hebrew monotheism comes to coincide — in a way that at first appears paradoxical — with the Christian confession of the Trinity. . . .

The Spirit of Life

Between Jesus' exodus to the Father and the disciples' exodus towards the fulfillment of history in God, there is the mission of the Spirit; it completes, and makes present in time, the mission of the Son: "I have said these things to you while I am still with you. But the Advocate, the Holy Spirit, whom the Father will send in my name, will teach you everything and remind you of all that I have said to you" (John 14:25-26).

The mission of the Word would be ineffective without the mission of the Consoler, who is not only the living memory of the Word, but who — precisely thanks to this role — is the One who "will guide you into all the truth; for he will not speak on his own, but will speak whatever he hears, and he will declare to you the things that are to come" (John 16:13). The Spirit is not the Word: yet he makes possible our life-giving encounter with the Word. Nor is he the Silence: yet he proclaims what he has heard from the Word in the eternal, divine silences, and opens for us the way into the future, entirely turned as he is towards the fullness of truth, which will be the eloquent silence of God, all in all (cf. 1 Cor. 15:28).

Thanks to the Spirit, the Word who is the Son and the Silence who is the Father meet in the human heart: one could say that the Spirit is the other silence, not of the origins, but that silence where the Word speaks and is at rest, so as then to go and be at peace in the silence of home, in the deep silences of God, after making the journey for which as Word he was sent out. So it is that the New Testament presents the Spirit in two ways: first, as the One who "opens" the divine, making possible the painful self-giving of the cross, by which God places himself in solidarity with the godless (cf. John 19:30); and, second, as the One who "unites" what is separated and divided, because at the Passover he unites the Father to the Son and, in the Son, to sinners, reconciled in the blood of the Crucified One (cf. Rom. 1:4; Eph. 2:13ff.). The approaches to the Holy Spirit that characterize respectively the Eastern and Western traditions of the Christian faith take their inspiration from this twofold work of the Consoler.

The Spirit, Bond of Divine Love

Western theology emphasizes the Spirit's role as the personal bond of unity between the Father and the Son. This emphasis originates in the concern to witness to the mysterious quality of the unity of the Christian God, over against the Greek idea of the One as separate and different from the many. In the data of revelation, the West discerns the Spirit's deep, indwelling work of reconciliation and peace, wrought at the raising of the crucified and when the Spirit is poured out on all flesh to reconcile sinners with God.

Spirit of communion, who founds the unity of the gifts in the one body of the Lord, which is the church (cf. 1 Cor. 12:4), and pours God's love into our hearts (cf. Rom. 5:5), the Holy Spirit is understood as the love in the depths of God, given by the Lover and received by the Beloved. He is other than the Father, because received by the Son, and other than the Son, because given by the Father; and yet he is one with them, because he is love given and received in the unity of eternal, living love: "The Spirit is an ineffable communion of the Father and Son."[13]

"Vinculum caritatis aeternae," bond of eternal love, the Spirit is at one and the same time the One who unites Lover and Beloved, and is also distinct from them as a specific person: "Whether he is in fact the unity of the one and the other, or their holiness, or their love, whether he is their unity because he is their love, or whether he is their love because he is their holiness, it is clear that he is not one or other of the two. In him, the one and the other are joined, and in him the one who is generated is loved by, and loves, the one who generates."[14]

This is the context where there emerges the idea that the Spirit proceeds from the Father and the Son (the "Filioque"); that he springs from their eternal dialogue of love, from their face-to-face encounter, which is a gift freely given and received, which is gratitude, shared fruitfulness, and mutual acceptance: "If in fact everything the Son has, he has from the Father, he also receives from the Father the fact that the Spirit proceeds also from him. By the gift the Father makes of the Spirit to the Son without any interval of time, the Spirit proceeds both from the one and the other."[15] Latin theology will make this way of looking at things its own, thus making up for the silence of the Nicene-Constantinopolitan Creed in this regard. This insight bears eloquent witness to the breadth and depth with which the theological understanding of the Spirit as the

13. St. Augustine, *De Trinitate* 5.11.12; PL 42:919.
14. St. Augustine, *De Trinitate* 6.5.7; PL 42:928.
15. St. Augustine, *De Trinitate* 15.26.47; PL 42:1095f.

unity and peace between Beloved and Lover has marked the spirituality and faith-reflection of the West. It is, then, "in the eternal mystery of God's being that we must look for the reason why no one can come to the Father except through the Son; why the Spirit, through whom the Father attracts humankind to Himself, is also from all eternity the Spirit of the Son; and why it is through the Spirit that the Father allows us to share in the divine sonship of Christ."[16]

Eastern criticisms of the "Filioque" have often blamed it for the exaggerated emphasis the West has given to the visible element in the church's life — in the understanding of the sacraments ("ex opere operato") and in moral objectivism and legalism. Even if these Eastern criticisms can at times themselves be somewhat exaggerated, there nevertheless seems to be some justification for the concern that the "Filioque" may lead to the attribution of an almost exclusive role to the Word, leaving the "monarchy" of the Father — the only source of divine life — in the shadows. While it is necessary, therefore, not to abandon the legitimate emphasis on the Word, it is no less necessary to relate the Word, on the one hand, to his origin, and, on the other, to his repose and home, in that encounter in which he proclaims and celebrates the glory of the Father. It is here that the West can be enriched by integration with the Eastern tradition, just as the latter can find in the witness of the West a stimulus to affirm and live the centrality of the Word.

The Spirit: "Ecstasy" of God

Eastern theology stresses how the Spirit exercises the role of "openness" in the relationship between the Father and the Son: he is in person the gift of love, the ecstasy of Lover and Beloved, their going out from self to give themselves to the other in time and eternity. This theology finds its starting point in the scriptural witness that every exodus of God from himself and into human history has been, and always will be, achieved in the Spirit. From creation (Gen. 1:2) to prophecy, from the incarnation of the Word (Matt. 1:18-20; Luke 1:35) to the birth of the church (Acts 2:1-13) — in all these, the East has perceived the movement of the unconditional self-giving of eternal love. In this sense, the Spirit proceeds from the Fa-

---

16. K. Barth, *Die kirchliche Dogmatik*, I/2 (Zürich: Evangelischer Verlag, 1942), p. 273.

ther, source of all divinity, through and outwards from the Son, in the way attested to by the events of salvation. For the East, to affirm that the Spirit also proceeds from the Son seems to place at risk the "monarchy" of the Father, his being the absolute beginning in divine silence.

It is, therefore, the Father who is understood as pouring out the Spirit on the Generated One, who in his turn — having given the Spirit over to the One who abandons him on the cross, and received that Spirit from the Father again in the fullness of Easter — gives the same Spirit to all flesh. The idea that the Consoler is the ecstasy and gift of God is expressed by the Greek fathers in the very frequently recurring formula: "From the Father, through the Son, in the Spirit." This "expresses a dynamic movement by which the Spirit is the One in whom the process ends. . . . It is a movement that takes place in events, but which nevertheless also reflects the dynamic life of the Trinity in itself. In this approach, the Spirit is understood as the One through whom God brings to fulfillment the communication of himself. To him are attributed the works of sanctification and perfection. In the Triune God he is the fulfillment. . . ."[17] In this way, the Spirit is perceived as the superabundance of divine love, the generous, free, and overflowing fullness of irradiating communion; he is the creator Spirit, gift of the Most High, source and contagious fire of life (cf. the Western hymn *Veni Creator*).

"The Spirit disturbs, as it were, the potential self-sufficiency of the 'face-to-face' dialogue of the first two persons. Christian Tradition has attributed to him a creative and dynamic role; in this sense, he is the One who provokes new differences. He is the openness of God's communion to what is not divine. He is the habitation of God there where God is, in a sense, 'away himself.' This is why he is called 'love.' He is the 'ecstasy' of God towards his 'other,' the creature. This third person of the Trinitarian communion excludes the possibility of a 'narcissistic' understanding of the relationship between the first two persons: God is the One who is open, he is communication, he is the source of life, of sharing."[18]

What are the consequences of this way of understanding the Spirit as exodus and gift? The fundamental consequence is that Word and Silence do not exhaust themselves the one in the other: their reciprocal encounter is neither possessive nor static, but open, overflowing, the dynamic

---

17. Y. Congar, *Credo nello Spirito Santo*, vol. 3 (Brescia: Queriniana, 1983), pp. 154f.
18. C. Duquoc, *Un Dio diverso* (Brescia: Queriniana, 1978), p. 117.

movement of a love which radiates outwards. The peculiar characteristic of the divine encounter, personal and unifying in the highest degree, is always to be open. We could say that in God the Spirit achieves the condition of true love, its freedom from possessiveness and jealousy: "Love is not standing there gazing into one another's eyes, but looking together towards the same goal" (Antoine de Saint-Exupéry).

The "co-beloved" (cf. Richard of St. Victor) of the love of Father and Son, the "third" person when their reciprocal self-giving and self-receiving meet, is, precisely in his distinctiveness and personal consistency, the proof that eternal love does not shut Lover and Beloved in the circle of their mutual exchange, but leads them to communion in a fruitfulness that transcends themselves. Their eternal encounter thus reveals the transcendence of eternal love: how it gives itself freely to the other, how it shares itself, and is thus the source of communication between persons, in the interplay of relationships between the divine persons and of their relationship with creatures, whom they have called into existence.

The eternal Spirit is thus the permanent mutual openness of the silence of the Father and of the Word, the one to the other. This is why he is the death of silence in the Word, and of the Word in the silence of ecstasy; why, that is, he is the One who proceeds from the Father for the Son, in his life as the eternal silence's eternal speech and the Word's silence; he is the silent Word over against the Word that speaks, and the eloquent silence over against the pure silence of the origin, from whom the Word proceeds. The eternal encounter is the immanent foundation in God of the necessity that the salvific work of the Word be completed by the salvific work of the Spirit: the Word offered in time is not everything. "I tell you the truth: it is to your advantage that I go away, for if I do not go away, the Advocate will not come to you; but if I go, I will send him to you" (John 16:7).

Revelation — free and generous presence of the divine mystery in history — is not only Word, not only silence, nor simply the two together. If revelation were only Word, it would not give access to the hidden depths of silence; if it were only silence, it would not be able to communicate with human beings, who encounter each other through language; if it were simply Word *and* silence, it would still lack their mutual self-transcendence in the encounter wrought by the Spirit. In that encounter, the Word says himself in the silence of deeds of life transformed by his coming, and silence is reached by way of the Word, contemplated by the heart, and in theological discourse. To encounter the Word means opening oneself to silence and listening deeply to it; to encounter silence means welcoming the Word and living that Word in the transparency of deeds.

Revelation in the Holy Spirit thus means encountering both Word and silence: and this so as to speak the Word in the silent simplicity of an existence redeemed, and to take nourishment from silence in a life lived contemplatively, the only place where the Word can speak in all its power. Whoever meets God in the Spirit who communicates himself in the events of revelation, shares in the unity of the Trinity, a unity that does not diminish the richness of the persons or cancel their differences. Such persons are drawn into the movement of outgoing love, which is the ecstasy of God from self, so that they too may live "ecstatically," turned towards their God.

In the power of the Spirit, revelation — which came to fulfillment in the time of the fullness of the Word — is made present to all times, ever old and ever new. In this way, transcendence and openness, proper of any encounter with God, lead to a growing understanding of what has already been given, to a perception of what is hidden in what is revealed, and this unleashes limitless energies of light and life: "When the Spirit of truth comes, he will guide you into all the truth; for he will not speak on his own, but will speak whatever he hears, and he will declare to you the things that are to come. He will glorify me, because he will take what is mine and declare it to you. All that the Father has is mine. For this reason I said that he will take what is mine ands declare it to you" (John 16:13-15).

"Spirit of truth": Spirit, that is, of God's fidelity to every epoch of human history, and hence Spirit of encounter, making possible contact and exchange with the mystery communicated in the Word proceeding from silence. This Consoler proclaims the truth of the Son — "he will take what is mine and declare it to you" — but, in and through this truth, he also proclaims the truth of the Father. In the Word, the Spirit opens the way to silence; in the silence, he causes the Word to speak; he is the encounter between them in eternity and in time, condition of the possibility in God of every salvific encounter between human beings and the revelation of the Word and silence. And if, in God, encounter is the unity of life and death in favor of life, this will be no less the case when this encounter is shared with human beings: it will mean exodus from self to welcome the Other and to give oneself to him; it will mean death to make room for the life that comes. The encounter of the human heart with the Word and with silence is achieved in an analogous unity of death and life in favor of life. It is the encounter with God, who is a consuming fire (cf. Deut. 4:24; Isa. 33:14; Heb. 12:29): it is the experience of the Spirit, to whom the church calls out: "Come, Holy Spirit, fill the hearts of your faithful, and enkindle in them the fire of your love!"

Trinity — Eternal Story of Love

Lover, Beloved, and Love

On Easter Day the Father's initiative is revealed; he is the God who constitutes Jesus his Son Christ and Lord "with power according to the Spirit of holiness by resurrection from the dead" (Rom. 1:4). These words draw us deep into the very mystery of the divine: beginning from all that has been revealed in the story of the One who loved his Son Jesus, and us in him, we can set out towards the eternal story of his love.

The events of our salvation point us to the inner life of the mystery: the Easter event is a sign, an intensely meaningful evocation of the divine life that is revealed, but not resolved, in the story of the cross and of the resurrection understood as the story of Trinitarian love. Starting from the fact that in revelation the initiative in love always lies with the Father, what stands out above all is how the Father's love is like a fountain: the Father is the beginning, source, and origin of divine life. Augustine calls him "totius Trinitatis principium" — "the beginning of the whole Trinity." This way of putting things expresses how absolutely free and unconditional the Father's love is; he has always loved, and will always love. Without any necessity, cause, or extrinsic reason he loves, and will always continue to love. He will never betray his loving fidelity: "God does not love us because we are good and beautiful, but he makes us good and beautiful by loving us" (Luther). We may thus speak of the absolute spontaneity and sovereignty, the inexhaustible creativity, of God's love. The Father is the eternal source of love, loving in absolute freedom; he is the eternal Lover, characterized by a love with no conditions whatsoever.

If the source of love is in the Father, in the Son we find receptivity to love. The Son is pure acceptance, eternal loving obedience, infinite gratitude: he is the one "loved . . . before the foundation of the world" (John 17:24), in whom the divine life flows in time and eternity, springing from the fullness of the Father: "Just as the Father has life in himself, so he has granted the Son also to have life in himself" (John 5:26). The eternal Lover is distinct from the eternally Beloved, who proceeds from the Lover through the overflowing fullness of his love: the Son is the Other in love, the One in whom there comes to rest the movement of infinite generosity of the source of Love.

The Lover is the beginning of the Beloved: from Love-the-source there springs Love-that-receives, in the unbounded unity of eternal Love. In the Christian tradition, this process, by which the One who lives in love gives origin in indissoluble unity to the One who receives and welcomes love, is called "generation": the eternal act of this eternal process is the eternal birth of the Son, his coming from the bosom of the Father. In relation to him who is beginning and source, eternally loving Love, the Son is the one generated, the eternally beloved: he is the Word of the Father. The Father is not a despot who crushes the Son, but a loving Father! The Son is not a mere cipher, an empty form where the absolutely Divine can communicate itself; he is the Beloved, the eternal Son, the chosen, the only-begotten.

In God, the receptivity of love has eternal value: to accept love is no less personalizing than giving love: letting yourself be loved is love, no less than loving. . . . Receiving too is divine! Precisely inasmuch as he is receptive Love, in the process of his eternal generation the Son is the immanent foundation of the absolutely free and unconditional self-communication that God achieves when he creates the world. Only the infinite receptivity of the Son, through whom and for whom all things have been created (Col. 1:16), and who entered into solidarity with sinners to the point of going into the exile of being accursed and of dying, allows the creature to accept the pure gift of being (the creation of the world) and of living in love, which is the new life of grace: in the Word all things have been created and everything is redeemed; in him we are offered the grace of the Father!

In this eternal story, the expression of the unbounded freedom with which God loves, the Spirit also has his place. He unites the One who is generated to the One who generates, showing how the indelible distinction of love does not mean separation. He is the communion of Lover and Beloved, who also ensures the communion of the eternal Lover with his creatures and with their stories of suffering, not apart from the Beloved, but precisely in and through him. The Spirit ensures that unity is stronger than distinction, and eternal joy stronger than the suffering caused by the non-love of creatures. Poured out on the Crucified One on Easter Day, he reconciles the Father with the Son abandoned on Good Friday and, in him, with the passion of the world. He is the Spirit of unity, of consolation, of peace and joy. The distinction between Father and Son is taken up into the higher unity of the love that proceeds from the Father and, resting on and reflected in the Son, returns to its origin without origin: the Spirit is the bond of eternal love. Thus the Father remains the beginning, the Son the expression, the Spirit their personal bond in the movement of divine eternity.

We can discern here the other role of the Spirit in the relationship between Father and Son: if in their distinction he is the personal bond of communion, himself distinct both from the one and the other because given by the one and received by the other, other than the Father because received by the Son, and other than the Son because given by the Father, in their communion he is the "condilectus" (Richard of St. Victor), beloved of the one and the other, their friend, distinct from the Father because friend of the Son, and distinct from the Son because friend of the Father. In this sense, the eternal movement which from the Father moves to the Son, and through the Son moves to the Spirit, in which the Father loves the Son in the Spirit, and the Son receives from the Father the love with which to love him in the same Spirit, speaks of the openness of Trinitarian love, its pure self-giving: this is why revelation shows us a God who always moves out of himself in the Spirit, both in creation and in redemption.

In this sense the Spirit brings the truth of divine love to completion, showing how love — if it is really that — is never closed or possessive, but open, a gift, an exodus from the circle of the two. The Spirit is the "ecstasy" of God towards his "other." In the Spirit, Lover and Beloved "open" towards one another in otherness, in the inner life of their mystery, as in the work of salvation: inasmuch as he is beyond the Son in the unbounded unity of love, the Spirit is also that personal place where God's story passes into human history, and human history into God's. . . .

The Unity of the Living God

So what happens at Easter reveals the history of God as Trinity. This is not only, that is, the story of the Father, Son, and Spirit, as they reveal the life-giving way they relate to each other, and the marvelous generosity of their love for the world. It is also the story of the unlimited unity of the Three who make history: both unity in indelible differentiation (at the cross) and in deepest communion (at Easter). It is the one story of the Love who hands over the Beloved (the Father), the Love who lets himself be handed over in absolute freedom (the Son), and the Love who, handed over to make it possible for God to enter into the exile of sinners, is poured out fully at Easter to lead sinners into the unifying and life-giving homeland of divine love (the Spirit). The unity of Easter is the unity of Love that loves (the Father), is loved (the Son), and unites in freedom (the Spirit). Here is revealed how love not only creates unity, but already presupposes it; how it is not so much a question of bringing strangers together, as a reunion of persons who in some sense drew apart from each other out of love for the world, and who now return from this exile to the original and ever renewed unity of the homeland.

Besides, the whole of Jesus' mission and work is accomplished thus: in his unity, pre-existent and eternal, with the Father and the Spirit. He who receives and gives the Spirit is the Son of God one with the Father, who by his resurrection establishes the unity of humankind in the unity of God the Trinity: "On that day (when the Spirit is poured out: cf. vv. 16 and 17) you will know that I am in my Father, and you in me, and I in you. . . . Those who love me will be loved by my Father, and I will love them and reveal myself to them. . . . Those who love me will keep my word, and my Father will love them, and we will come to them and make our home with them" (John 14:20-21, 23). ". . . That they may all be one. As you, Father, are in me and I am in you, may they also be in us, so that the world may believe that you have sent me. . . . I in them and you in me, that they may become completely one, so that the world may know that you have sent me and have loved them even as you have loved me" (John 17:21, 23). This Trinitarian unity, revealed and shared at Easter, was vigorously affirmed by the faith of the church against those who wanted to deny or dilute it: the declaration of the Council of Nicea (325) about the "consubstantiality" of the Son with the Father affirms that they are on the same plane of divine being, one in divinity, of one and the same "essence." In 381 the Council of Constantinople, responding to those who were tending to subordinate the Spirit to Christ, affirmed the same equality of divine being of the Spirit with the Father and the Son, with whom he is "adored and glorified" as Lord and giver of life.

Starting from that revelation of love that loves, is loved, and unites in freedom, which is the story of Easter, God's unity may be understood as pure love, underpinning the indelible Trinitarian distinction of Lover, Beloved, and Love in person. As Augustine wrote: "In truth you see the Trinity, if you see love."[19] "Behold they are three: Lover, Beloved, and Love."[20] "And not more than three: one who loves the one who comes from him, one who loves the one he comes from, and love itself. . . . And if this is nothing, how is God love? And if this is not substance, how is God substance?"[21] So the essence of the living God is his love in the eternal dynamism of exodus from self, as loving Love; of welcoming self, as beloved Love; of return to self and of infinite openness to the other in freedom, as Spirit of Trinitarian Love.

The essence of the Christian God is love in eternal movement, the Trinitarian story of love, the Trinity as the eternal story of love, which calls forth, takes up, and pervades the history of the world, the object of its pure love. What happened at Easter does not reveal the divine essence in any other way than as the eternal event of love between the three and their love for us. The unity of God is thus the unity of his being-love, of his essential love, which exists eternally as loving Love, beloved Love, and personal Love; as eternal source, advent, and future of Love; as origin, acceptance, and gift; as fatherhood, sonship, and openness in freedom; as Father, Son, and Holy Spirit.

This understanding of the essential unity of the living God as the eternal story of love is expressed by the idea of Trinitarian "perichoresis": on the basis of scriptural affirmations like John 10:38 — "the Father is in me and I am in the Father" — the expression is used to express the mutual inhabitation of the divine persons, the inexhaustible movement of the Trinitarian life, its continual unfolding and gathering in love. "The fact that the three Persons remain and live the one in the other," writes St. John Damascene, "means that they are inseparable and cannot

---

19. St. Augustine, *De Trinitate* 8.8.12; PL 42:959.
20. St. Augustine, *De Trinitate* 8.10.14; PL 42:960.
21. St. Augustine, *De Trinitate* 6.5.7; PL 42:928.

be detached from one another, and they live in this way without confusion, so not in such a way that they become one or confused, but that they are united. . . . One and identical is the movement, because the thrust and the dynamism of the three Persons is unique, and this is something that cannot be observed in created nature."[22] The beauty and depth of this vision lie in the fact that — while it refuses every conception of the divine life that might exaggerate unity against distinction (modalism), or personal distinction against unity (tritheism) — it shows how in the living God the unity and originality of the persons are not only not in competition, but affirm each other reciprocally. The divine essence as love does not exclude, but includes personal differences: and this goes as much for the immanence of the divine life, as for the mystery of this life shared with humankind. Divine love does not cancel differences, even if it takes them up into a unity deeper than themselves. . . .

One can then understand how this vision of Trinitarian love has the sound of good news in the age of the crisis of the ideologies and of the loneliness of nihilism. In ideological totalitarianism there is no room for difference: and this absence inexorably produces violence, alienation, and death. The same, however, happens in postmodern nihilism, which does not tolerate otherness so much as it tends to destroy it or reduce it to the mere appearance of the same in the general triumph of solitude. Against the ideological concern for the masses over against the individual, the gospel of the Trinity recalls the infinite dignity of each human being. Against nihilism, it proclaims the real possibility of the encounter with the other and the victory over loneliness, thanks to the dialogue and communion made possible by that love which constitutes the essential unity of the living God. In both cases, it is the good news of Trinitarian communion which is the true response to the deepest needs emerging from the crisis of our present age: we become capable of love when we discover that we are loved first, enfolded and led by the strength of a love that does not cancel differences, indeed giving them value in unity. Enfolded by eternal love, welcomed into the Trinitarian story of love, human beings can build stories of love in the truth of their lives.

The love of the Trinitarian God is thus the good news that responds to the truest needs of our times and hearts. Nothing that we ourselves create, or that remains merely on the human plane, can save us from our

22. St. John Damascene, *De Fide Orthodoxa* 1.14; PG 94:860.

loneliness. This loneliness, indeed, will increase as we discover who we are, because it is nothing other than the obverse of the communion to which we are called. Once this communion has gone missing, there remains a loneliness that has the same width and depth. Only God can respond to this infinite expectation, he who "made us to be brought together into the heart of the life of the Trinity. . . . There is a place where this gathering-together of all things in the Trinity begins in this world; 'a family of God', a mysterious extension of the Trinity in time, which not only prepares us for this life of union and gives us a sure guarantee of it, but also makes us participate in it already. The Church is the only completely 'open' society, the only one which measures up to our deepest longings, and in which we can finally find our whole shape. . . . That is the Church."[23] To this church the revelation of the Trinity leads us as to the Trinity's habitation in time, its sign raised among us, even if still in the fragility of this world that passes and in our unquenchable thirst for the eternal, which will never be fully slaked. . . .

23. H. de Lubac, *The Splendor of the Church*, trans. Michael Mason (San Francisco: Ignatius, 1986), p. 238.

· III ·

Living in Christ and the Church

How can revelation, brought to completion in Jesus' threefold exodus, speak to the crisis provoked by the collapse of the false certainties offered by the ideologies, and to the painful lack of reasons for a great hope so typical of postmodern nihilism? To respond adequately to this question we must show how Christians, engaged in living and working in this changing world, are required more than ever today to give an account of the hope that is in them, with gentleness and respect for all (cf. 1 Peter 3:15), and so to become a place where the Other is present in history.

At both individual and community levels, this means that Christians must be disciples of the Only One, servants out of love, and witnesses to what it means to follow the Lord in his threefold exodus. At the same time, in the interplay between faith and nonbelief — to which the adventures of modern atheism and the restlessness of nihilistic postmodernism make us especially attentive — believers are called to go beyond every reduction of Christianity to ideology, and to be sincerely attentive to others in all their dignity, whatever their beliefs may be.

Thus it is that we discover that the atheist, the only atheist that can be taken seriously, may live in the very heart of believers themselves, because only someone who believes in God, and has experienced his "impossible" love, can also "know" what it would mean to deny him, and what infinite suffering his absence would be. The nonbeliever, that is, is not outside believers, but within them: this insight leads to a particular understanding of the life of faith itself, lived now not presumptuously, as something possessed, but in humble awareness of the ever new need to put oneself at the service of the truth, and to do this not as so many private adventurers, but in the indispensable communion of the church of love, which has been raised up and is nourished by the Spirit. In this special call to service, faith and history come together in the Trinity, which is understood as origin, guardian, and home of the world, transcendent and adorable womb in which we live and move and have our being, and where we must find inspiration, in the most concrete of ways, for our deeds and days.

The Threefold Exodus of the Disciple

Disciples of the Only One: Giving Faith First Place

Faced with the collapse of meaning, with the postmodern refusal even to ask the question of meaning, those who believe in Christ are called, above all, to place him at the center of their hearts as the meaning of their lives, perceiving themselves as disciples of the Only One, revealed in him, and searching passionately after the truth about the living God who frees and saves. As the Son lived his exodus from the Father while remaining totally immersed in the silence of the origins, and drawing all things into relationship with the Other, so those who respond to his call — "Come, follow me" — are called to live hidden with Christ in God (cf. Col. 3:3).

The Word made flesh — accepted in faith — makes the disciple into a person who receives everything from God and who gives God first place in everything. This is how believers can proclaim by their lives that there are reasons to live, and to live together. As Jesus showed by his exodus from the Father, these reasons are not to be found only in ourselves or in this world, but outside of us, in the Other who comes to us, in that ultimate horizon which faith recognizes as revealed and given in Christ. So faith leads us to affirm the primacy of God, and hence the first place to be given to the contemplative dimension of life, understood as faithful union with Christ in God, having at heart what is eternal, towards which he has opened the way for us. We are called to live in the vibrant memory of the God-with-us, risking our entire life for him in the self-abandonment of faith.

This is the same faith lived by the Son who came in the flesh, whose existence among us — as the Letter to the Hebrews affirms — was spent in total obedience to the Father: "In the days of his flesh, Jesus offered up prayers and supplications, with loud cries and tears, to the one who was able to save him from death, and he was heard because of his reverent submission. Although he was a Son, he learned obedience through what he suffered: and having been made perfect, he became the source of eternal salvation for all who obey him" (Heb. 5:7-9).

In his exodus from God, Jesus reveals himself as truly the "pioneer and perfecter of our faith" (Heb. 12:2), who has gone before us and who strengthens us in our struggle to believe and to abandon ourselves into God's hands. In Christians' union with him, they learn to place their own lives in the hands of the Other, so that he may be their one true Lord. Believing means letting yourself, in union with Christ, fall prisoner to the unseen God; it means letting yourself be possessed by him, in obedient attention to his Word and silence. In the life of a disciple, the acceptance of revealed truth is joined to free submission to grace and to trust in God's promises, where faith is lived as personal encounter and unconditional self-abandonment to God.

In this life of faith, we continually receive our own life from the Father's hands and, at the same time, we hand ourselves over in self-abandonment to his truth and love, following Jesus, who — "coming forth" from God — never stopped living with the life of his God and Father. It is this exodus that makes us free: free from ourselves, free from the seduction of possession and the obsessive search for human security. To believe, therefore, does not mean avoiding scandal or fleeing risk: we believe, not despite scandal and risk, but precisely challenged by and in them.

To believe means to confess God's love even when there is no evidence of this love. It means hoping against all hope, accepting the crucifixion of our own expectations on Christ's cross, and not crucifying Christ on the cross of these very expectations. To believe means drawing near to God in fear and trembling, removing our sandals, ready to recognize his presence not in wind, fire, and earthquake, but in the "sound of sheer silence," like Elijah on the holy mountain — just as it has been, is, and always will be for all the saints and prophets (cf. 1 Kings 19:11-13).

Thus totally dependent on the Father, believers become aware of their own relativity: as individuals and as a community, they recognize that they are not an absolute but an instrument, not an end but a means, entirely relative to the primacy of God, poor servants and pilgrims. No possession, no success, must extinguish in them this passionate hope: every claim to have already arrived, every "ecstasy of fulfillment," is a temptation and a hindrance. The community of Christ's disciples is not yet the glorious Kingdom, but only the Kingdom that has begun, present in mystery ("praesens in mysterio": *Lumen Gentium, 3*). It bears within it the passing nature of this world, and lives through the groans and birth pangs of the new heavens and new earth. Every identification of the Kingdom with one or other earthly reality is to be rejected: the church — docile to the breath of the Spirit — is on the way and not yet at home, and is therefore "semper reformanda," called to unceasing renewal and to continual purification.

In the marvel of attentiveness and praise, in the service of charity, in the proclamation of the Word, in the celebration of the sacraments, the community of disciples knows it must let itself be possessed ever more by its Spouse, to "tend incessantly towards the fullness of the divine truth, in order that in it there may reach fulfillment the words of God" (*Dei Verbum,* 8). Nothing is further removed from the life of faith than an attitude of triumphalism, or of submission to the seduction of this world's power and possessions. The disciple's final goal is not self-affirmation by human standards of greatness, but instead, like old Simeon, to sing the "Nunc dimittis" when the light of the nations has risen for all. In this way, Christian witness will be clothed in light, and attract all the world's peoples to walk towards their Lord. . . .

Servants out of Love, Charity Their Mark

Following Jesus, who lives his exodus from self till the point of handing himself over on the cross, Christians are called to become *servants out of love.* This call is more urgent than ever today, in this time of loneliness and refusal to love, often influenced by postmodern nihilism. Christians proclaim Christ, above all, by living their exodus from self without return, following his example, in solidarity especially with their weakest and poorest companions on the road, to whom Christ made himself a neighbor.

If Christ is the center of the disciple's life, if he is the one on whom the Christian "hangs," conquered by his cross, enlightened by his resurrection, then no disciple of Jesus will be able to draw back from the history of suffering and tears into which Christ came, and where he planted his cross so as to extend the power of his Easter victory. The disciples of the Truth who saves are never alone: they are with him, at the service of their neighbor, living as companions of God-with-us. The task entrusted to them by the Master will not be fulfilled, humankind's promised future will not be built, by fleeing from the responsibilities of service. The world that has emerged from the shipwreck of ideological totalitarianism has more need than ever of that down-to-earth, discreet charity and solidarity, which know how to express themselves in true companionship, and how to build the way forward in communion, reflecting Christ the Savior's light.

The disciples of the Crucified One must demonstrate the audacity of meaningful deeds clearly inspired by charity, as they follow him, abandoned to die for us — deeds that give credibility to the words they proclaim and fill them with his deep, divine silence. In the midst of the widespread contemporary skepticism about the possibility of truly loving, it is today more important than ever to proclaim the good news of God's love, the joyful and transforming message that God "so loved the world that he gave his only Son, so that everyone who believes in him may not perish but may have eternal life" (John 3:16), and that the Son has loved us and given himself for us, thus making us able to love (cf. Gal. 2:20). If God revealed himself as love when Jesus went out of himself to be abandoned on the cross, he will also reveal himself as love in the disciple who is free from self to the point of offering the supreme gift of love: "No one has ever seen God; if we love one another, God lives in us, and his love is perfected in us" (1 John 4:12). To share in this love is the gift the Spirit makes to our hearts: "God's love has been poured into our hearts through the Holy Spirit that has been given to us" (Rom. 5:5).

So when we share in Jesus' exodus from self we experience what it means to be free in love, and thus free to give ourselves unconditionally. Free through faith, the Christian is a servant because of love. "Since God loved us so much, we also ought to love one another" (1 John 4:11). Just as God's love is motivated only by the irradiating joy of loving, so the disciple's charity is all the truer and more credible when it rejects calculation and self-interest, and is offered unconditionally in the exodus from self with no return: "Love is patient; love is kind; love is not envious or boastful or arrogant or rude. It does not insist on its own way; it is not irritable or resentful; it does not rejoice in wrongdoing, but rejoices in the truth. It bears all things, believes all things, hopes all things, endures all things" (1 Cor. 13:4-7). One expression of this free self-giving is the love able to love others for themselves, and not to possess or enslave them: the sign of such love is the commitment to solidarity with the world's least and weakest. Today more than ever, as the sun goes down on the easy ideological solutions, and there is the insidious temptation of shutting ourselves up in our selfishness, charity towards the poor is the distinguishing mark of the Christian. And this love — intelligent, free, audacious — is inseparable from the experience of being hidden with Christ in God, knowing ourselves enfolded and guarded with Christ in the Father's love.

This all means that the disciple must know that the great things of this world have only a relative value: seen against the ultimate horizon revealed by hope in Christ, everything else appears "penultimate," subject to judgment by the Lord's promise, which is always alive and contemporary by the power of the Spirit. Christians live in history under the sign of exile and struggle; as the Second Vatican Council says: "'While we are at home in the body we are away from the Lord' (2 Cor. 5:6) and having the first fruits of the Spirit we groan inwardly (cf. Rom. 8:23) and we desire to be with Christ (cf. Phil. 1:23). That same charity urges us to live more for him who died for us and rose again (cf. 2 Cor. 5:15). We make it our aim, then, to please the Lord in all things (cf. 2 Cor. 5:9), and we put on the armor of God that we may be able to stand against the wiles of the devil and resist in the evil day (cf. Eph. 6:11-13)" (*Lumen Gentium*, 48). When Christians follow Christ and become servants out of love, they will learn to be wary of every short-term fulfillment of this world's hopes. As they seek to be present in every human situation, in solidarity with the poor and oppressed, it will never be legitimate for them to identify their hope with one of the hopes at play in history. This style of service will also mean Christians have to take a position on denouncing injustice: to love people in a real way can also mean subverting the way they think and act. It comes down to giving first place not to worldly agendas or political calculation, but to a concern only for the cause of the truth of Jesus Christ, and of his justice; it involves risking one's life in his name, committing one's life through witness, carrying the cross, while always striving to find a way forward in communion with all.

Witnesses to Meaning: Reasons for Hope

Christians are disciples of the One who lived the exodus from self till the point of handing himself over on the cross: as such, faced with the contemporary lack of hope and passion for the truth, they are called to witness to the meaning of life and history. They are called to love the home revealed by Christ's resurrection, and to stand ready to pay the price of fidelity to this homeland in the daily struggle with all that is penultimate: only thus can they be witnesses of hope for others. Christians must rediscover in full the passion for truth revealed in Christ: there they will find the truest foundation for their witness as pilgrims journeying towards the homeland. To love the truth means to fix our gaze on the fulfillment of God's promise in Christ, who died and rose for us, and to be ready to pay the price for this truth at every step we take. This is the fidelity required if our witness to hope is to be credible and not to disappoint. We have to have the consciences of adults, desiring to please God in all things, ready to demonstrate in every choice we make the relevance of the greater meaning of life and history.

Faith and charity — lived respectively in union with the exodus of Jesus from the Father and with the exodus of Jesus from himself — are thus one with hope, the mark in the disciple of the exodus of Jesus towards the Father, to which the disciple is united by the power of the Spirit: "hope does not disappoint us because God's love has been poured into our hearts through the Holy Spirit that has been given to us" (Rom. 5:5). In the disciples, the risen Christ is the hope of glory (cf. Col. 1:27), and the living God they proclaim is the God of hope, the source of joy and peace in the Spirit: "May the God of hope fill you with all joy and peace in believing, so that you may abound in hope by the power of the Holy Spirit" (Rom. 15:13). Christian hope is not a mere projection of the desires of our heart: given from above, it is rather an anticipation, the future of God already at work now in the heart of history. This is why Christian hope does not deny the human face of hope: human hopes, though, must be verified against the resurrection of the Lord, which, on the one hand, strengthens every authentic commitment to liberation and human promotion, and, on the other, contests every attempt to make human goals into an absolute.

In this twofold sense, hope of the resurrection is the resurrection of hope: it gives new life to whatever is imprisoned by death, and passes judgment on anything that sets itself up as an idol in the human heart. Because of hope's "eschatological reservation" about everything that is not of ultimate significance, because, that is, of God's promise which fills Christians' hearts, they will not identify their faith with any ideology, party, or system. Instead, they must be the critical conscience of all of these, a reminder of our origin and ultimate goal, pressing so that the wholeness of the person may find fulfillment in every human being, according to the Father's plan.

Jesus' disciples will know how to be awkward and disquieting, everything other than tools of the powerful, or shut into a "spiritual" disdain for practical engagement. The goal revealed in Jesus' exodus towards the Father, while it makes Christians strangers and pilgrims in this world, is not a dream alienating them from reality, but a power urging them to commit themselves in the cause of justice, peace, and the integrity of creation in the contemporary world.

The new life generated in the encounter with the God of hope becomes visible above all in the choice of evangelical poverty. This is quite other than the alienation of abject misery; it is instead the condition of the "poor of the Lord," who place all their trust in God and act in consequence. Poverty means being open to the surprises of the Eternal, and so it also means refusing to manage one's life on one's own. Poverty means planning for and building the future of human beings, while giving God first place, knowing that he touches and transforms in freedom everything that lives. So to live the spirit of poverty means being open to the Eternal, free from self to belong to him, ready to let oneself be touched and troubled by his coming, ready to give up every security already attained, accepting to live by the ever surprising fidelity of God, who clothes the lilies of the field and feeds the birds of the air. Hope, then, is the sister of faith, and lives with the love that comes from God. In the unity of their new life in Christ, believers are called to wager their lives on the new horizon opened up by his resurrection; to live, that is, as disciples of Jesus, the truly free human being, who in his poverty lived with complete confidence in God, witnessing to the truth and beauty of being free from self, free for the Father and others, till the end, beyond every frontier.

In particular, in this postmodern age so lacking in hope, the lives of Jesus' disciples must be a vigorous foretaste of the joy of eternal life, victorious over suffering, evil, and death, promised in Christ's return to the

Father. Despite the trials and contradictions of the present, the people of God are called to exult in hope even now: in the community straining towards the goal disclosed to us in the Risen One, the word of the psalm finds fulfillment: "I was glad when they said to me, 'Let us go to the house of the Lord!'" (Ps. 122:1). The Christian's joy does not come from any claim of building a ladder up to heaven, a sort of new tower of Babel for a world imprisoned in itself: the peace and strength of Christian joy have their roots in the resurrection of the Humble One. He assures his disciples of true life both in time and beyond, giving them the certainty that the Spirit poured out by him is already at work building here and now the future promised by God. God "has time" for human beings and labors with them to build his house: Jerusalem, longed for and desired, comes down already into the heart of the human adventure: "The Spirit and the bride say, 'Come.' . . . The one who testifies to these things says, 'Surely, I am coming soon'" (Rev. 22:17-20). Of this desire, of this joyful and vigilant expectation, the disciple's life is called to become both a sign and a proclamation in the most various times and places of history. . . .

Faith, hope, and charity are, therefore, the characteristic expressions of the new life generated in the human heart when God's call and gift in Christ find a welcome there. This is already affirmed by the most ancient of the Christian scriptures, the Letter to the Thessalonians: "We always give thanks to God for all of you and mention you in our prayers, constantly remembering before our God and Father your work of faith and labor of love and steadfastness of hope in our Lord Jesus Christ" (1 Thess. 1:2-3). The entire existence of the Christian means living before the Father, following Jesus, by the grace of the Spirit, in faith, hope, and charity: "Since we have confidence to enter the sanctuary by the blood of Jesus, by the new and living way that he opened for us through the curtain (that is, through his flesh) . . . let us approach with a true heart in full assurance of faith, with our hearts sprinkled clean from an evil conscience and our bodies washed with pure water. Let us hold fast to the confession of our hope without wavering, for he who has promised is faithful. And let us consider how to provoke one another to love and good deeds" (Heb. 10:19-24). In sharing the threefold exodus of their Lord, Christians are called to believe, to love, to hope. This is who they are; this is their strength; and this is why they are humble. Here, in particular, there is the message that a redeemed existence can offer to this age of ours, lacking in hope and marked by loneliness.

Believing and Not Believing

The Atheism of the Believer

To believe is to be taken prisoner by the Totally Other. This is precisely why believers can bring the truth of faith to bear on human thought, as they let themselves become prisoners of the invisible, of the not immediately available and certain. Believing thought does not claim to have an explanation for everything, to throw light on everything, but lives rather as if by night, charged with expectation, suspended between the first and last coming, already strengthened, certainly, by the light that came into the darkness, and yet still longing for the dawn. Believing thought is not yet totally lit up by the day, which belongs to another time and to another homeland, but it still receives enough light to bear the burden of keeping the faith. Believing thought is humble; it hangs on the cross, which in the world's darkness is, and always will be, the disciple's guiding, redeeming star.

In their turn, nonbelievers, once they have crossed the ford of modernity, live in the selfsame state of search and expectation. This is on condition that their nonbelief is more than a label, that it is the fruit of their experience of suffering and struggle with God and of their being unable to believe in him. True nonbelief is not the adventure of a facile denial, leaving the person the way they were before. Serious, thoughtful nonbelief, which pays attention to the real questions, means suffering; it is a passion for truth that pays a personal price for the bitter courage of not believing.

This may be illustrated by a text that can be considered to mark the first appearance of the theme of the death of God in European awareness: the "Speech of the Dead Christ," written towards the end of the eighteenth century by the German romantic poet, Jean Paul Richter. It tells a story, which has all the power of a metaphor: "Once upon a time, one summer's evening, I was lying on a mountain-top, my face to the sun, and I fell asleep. I dreamt, and in my dream I awoke in a cemetery. . . . All the shadows of the dead were standing round the altar. . . . And behold there descended onto the altar a tall, noble figure, as if bearing the weight of a sorrow without end. And all the dead cried out: 'Christ! Is there no God?' He replied: 'No, there is not. . . . I have traversed the worlds, I have gone up to the suns, and flown along the milky ways and over the deserts of heaven; but there is no God. I went down to where there is only the shadow of being, and peered into the abyss and cried out: "Father, where are you?" But I only heard the sound of the eternal tempest which no one has mastered.' . . . Then into the temple came all the children who had died, and they threw themselves at the feet of the tall figure near the altar, saying: 'Jesus! Do we have no father?' . . . And everything became narrow, grim, anguished — and an enormous battering-ram was about to strike the last hour of time and to throw down the world's edifice . . . when I re-awoke. My soul wept with the joy of still being able to adore God — and this joy, and my tears and faith in Him, were my prayer."[1]

Written as the adventure of emancipated reason dawned, this text illustrates how not believing means being aware of the acute pain of absence, feeling irredeemably orphaned, completely abandoned: only the death of God can cause such sorrow in the human heart and in the history of the world. Thus it is that the thinking nonbeliever, just as the conscientious believer, wrestles with God. "My religion is to wrestle with God": according to Miguel de Unamuno, a voice speaking for the "tragic sentiment of life," the whole of religion lies in this "wrestling with God." And since "to live is to yearn for eternal life," living is inevitably marked by the tragedy of having to fight this unequal combat. Out of respect for this dignity of nonbelief, which emerged in all its clarity after the tragically heady days of ideological atheism and its fall, believers are called to question their faith and discover the abyss of nonbelief within them.

The company that faith and nonbelief keep one another in this way has its origins in the one human condition: when human beings ask the deepest questions about their inevitable vulnerability to pain and death, they do this not as people who have already arrived, but as searchers for the distant homeland, who let themselves be permanently called into question, provoked and seduced by the furthest horizon. Human beings who stop, who feel they have mastered the truth, for whom the truth is no longer Someone who possesses you more and more, but rather someone to be possessed, such persons have not only rejected God, but also their own dignity as human beings.

To be human is to go on a journey outwards: human beings are on an

---

1. Jean Paul Richter, "Discorso del Cristo morto," in *Scritti sul nichilismo,* a cura di Adriano Fabris (Brescia: Morcelliana, 1997), pp. 25-30.

exodus, called permanently to go out of themselves, to question themselves, in search of home, glimpsed but not possessed. . . . If human beings are by constitution pilgrims towards life, "begging for heaven" (Jacques Maritain), their real temptation is to stop journeying, to feel they have arrived, no longer to think of themselves as exiles in this world, but proprietors and masters of an impossible "eternal instant." This illusion of feeling that we have arrived, the presumption of thinking we are already fulfilled, that we have achieved the goal of our existence — this is the fatal illness.

All this can be applied analogously to the things of God: in the life of faith, too, the greatest temptation is to stop. Because Christians are called to follow the cross, where God spoke in the silent, disquieting eloquence of the passion, they are constantly placed before this great choice: to crucify their own expectations on the cross of Christ, or to crucify Christ on the cross of these expectations. This way of the cross is the gospel of freedom, as Jesus showed us in the way he went out of himself in choice after choice, till the point of deepest self-abandonment! In everyday experience, as in the journey of faith, human beings are called to be free by paying the painful price of this continual, inevitable choice, a choice that constantly places us on the threshold, sensing the dizzy alternative of going one way or the other. . . .

Faith: Struggle, Scandal, Submission

As human beings constantly go out of themselves to struggle against death and walk towards life, they are joined by the Word who comes from silence, from that God who — according to Christian faith — "has had time" for them. God comes from his eternal silence so our history may enter the silence of home and there find rest. This meeting between human beings who go out and God who comes, between exodus and advent, is faith. It is struggle and agony, not the repose of a certainty possessed. Whoever thinks they can have faith without a struggle risks believing in nothing. Faith is what happened to Jacob at the ford of Jabbok (cf. Gen. 32:23-33): God is the one who attacks under cover of dark, who comes upon you and wrestles with you. If you do not know God in this way, if for you God is not a consuming fire, if for you the encounter with him is always going through the same comfortable motions, your God has stopped being the living God, and is dead, a "Deus otiosus."

That is why Pascal said that Christ would be in agony until the end of time: his agony is the agony of Christians, the struggle to believe, to hope, to love, the struggle with God! God is other than you, he is free with respect to you — as you are other than him, and free with respect to him. Woe to us if we lose the sense of this distance and with it the suffering involved in our difference from God! In a beautifully naïf medieval insight, to believe *(credere)* comes from "cor-dare," to give your heart, and this involves a continual struggle with God's total otherness which does not let itself be "solved" or "possessed." God is other than you. That is why doubt will always inhabit faith.

Only those who do not know are shocked by the Baptist's words, when at the sunset of his life and evidently restless with doubt, sent to ask Jesus: "Are you the one who is to come, or are we to wait for another?" (Matt. 11:3). This is the trial of faith: to struggle with God, knowing that he is the Other, who escapes from our certainties, and does not allow himself to be tamed by our presumption. So faith is also scandal: the voices that witness to this are innumerable. St. John of the Cross speaks of this scandal through the ambivalent metaphor of the "noche oscura": "On a dark night/anguished, with burning love/oh blessed fate/I went out, unnoticed/all were asleep at home./.../Night, you led me!/oh, night more lovable than dawn/oh, night that joined/the Lover with his beloved/the beloved transformed into the Lover."[2]

Dark night is both the place of scandal and betrothal: God is not to be found in easy earthly possessiveness, but in the poverty of the cross, in death to self, in the night of the senses and of the spirit. This is the place of greatest joy! Writing at the beginning of the "short century" that will bear the bitterest fruits of ideology's presumption, St. Theresa of the Child Jesus is not afraid to name the scandal of faith with radical authenticity: "Jesus made me sense how there really do exist souls without faith. He allowed my soul to be invaded by the deepest darkness, so that the thought of heaven, so sweet to me, might become nothing other than

---

2. San Juan de la Cruz, *Noche oscura,* 1 and 5: "En una noche oscura,/con ansias, en amores inflamada,/¡oh dichosa ventura!,/salí sin ser notada,/estando ya mi casa sosegada./.../¡Oh noche que guiaste!/¡Oh noche amable más que el alborada!/¡Oh noche que juntaste/Amado con amada/amada en el Amadao transformada!"

struggle and torment. . . . You would have to journey in this darkness to understand what it means. . . ." Darkness is the place of love, and of faith experienced as struggle and scandal. Christ is not the answer to our questions; above all, he subverts them. And only after leading us into the fire of desolation does he becomes the God of consolation and of peace.

Finally, faith is submission: in the combat there comes the moment when you understand that the loser really wins, and so you give yourself up to him, you submit to the one who attacks at night, you allow your life to be marked forever by that meeting. Then it is that faith becomes self-abandonment and forgetfulness of self and the joy of entrusting yourself into the arms of the Beloved. Faith means entrusting yourself like this to the Other. "O Lord, you have enticed me, and I was enticed; you have overpowered me, and you have prevailed. . . . If I say, 'I will not mention him, or speak any more in his name, then within me there is something like a burning fire shut up in my bones; I am weary with holding it in, and I cannot" (Jer. 20:7-9). In these words of Jeremiah we hear the voice of one of the greatest witnesses to what it means to submit in faith: Jeremiah wrestled mightily with God, but in the midst of the combat he learned how to give in, to submit in love and to entrust himself to God. This is how faith can become a homecoming of beauty and peace. This is not the beauty the world knows, the seduction of a truth explaining everything; it is instead the beauty of the man of sorrows, the beauty of crucified Love, of Jesus' total offering of himself to the Father and to us.

If faith, then, is all this, if it is struggle, scandal, and submission inseparably joined, then believers will not be looking for vulgar signs that exhibit the fidelity of the God in whom they believe. They will still believe in him even when the answer to the real questions of human suffering stay hidden in his silence. Consequently, believers are, in the end, atheists who try every day to begin believing; and — we may perhaps say — nonbelievers, as they suffer from the infinite pain of God's absence, are believers who try anew every day to begin not to believe. If believers did not try every day to begin believing, their faith would be nothing more than worldly reassurance, one of the many ideologies that have fooled the world and alienated human beings. Against every ideology, faith is to be understood and lived as continual conversion to God, a continual handing over of the heart, beginning every day afresh the effort to believe, hope, and love: in consequence, faith is prayer, and those who do not pray will not live by faith!

But if believers are atheists who try every day to begin believing, then what of the atheists, the nonbelievers who have lived through the adventures of modernity and its crisis? Will they not perhaps be believers who live the opposite struggle — of trying not to believe? Not, of course, the superficial atheists, but those who struggle with an upright conscience, who have sought but not found, and who feel all the pain of God's absence: will they not be the brothers and sisters of those who believe?

From this way of looking at things we find that we are called to make some important distinctions. In the first place, to say "no" to a slovenly, lazy, static, habit-worn faith, made of comfortable intolerance, which defends itself by condemning others because it does not know how to live the suffering of love. To this "no" we must add a "yes" to a questioning, even doubting, faith, capable of beginning anew every day to entrust itself to others, to live the exodus with no return towards his silence, disclosed and hidden in his Word.

There also arises, however, a "no" to every superficial atheism, to every ideological denial of God and of the holy mystery, as well as a "yes" to the unceasing search for the hidden Face, for the silence beyond the Word and for the crucified Word, where silence opens itself to embrace our searching hearts. In this age of ours that lacks great hopes, perhaps more than ever the real difference is not between believers and nonbelievers, but between those who think and those who do not, between, on the one hand, men and women who have the courage to face life's pain, to go on trying to believe, hope, and love, and, on the other, men and women who have given up the struggle, who seem to content themselves with the penultimate horizon, and no longer know how to burn with desire and yearning at the thought of our last horizon and last home. Any deed whatsoever, even the most costly, is thus worth doing to set alight again this desire for our true home, and to give us the courage to journey there, till the end and beyond. . . .

Believers thus make their own — in the name, too, of nonbeliever — the prayer with which St. Augustine closes the most beautiful, the most deeply considered, and perhaps the most tormented of his works, the fifteen books of *De Trinitate:* "Lord my God, my only hope, grant that when I am weary I may never cease to seek You, but may always passionately seek Your face. Give me strength to seek You who let Yourself be encountered, and give me the hope of meeting You more and more. Before You I place my strength and my weakness: conserve the first, heal the last. Before You I place my knowledge and my ignorance; where You have opened, welcome me as I enter; where You have closed to me, open when I knock. Let me remember You, understand You, love You!"[3]

And perhaps for the same reasons the thoughtful nonbeliever becomes conscious of the fascinating paradox of the prayer he cannot stop himself from saying: "Grant us, O Lord, the paradises of nothingness, the gardens of your springtime. Lord, you make the night into a morning, the morning we pay for with the glittering coins of the stars, the stars of the night, guide of the wanderers, of the wanderers towards the infinite: what is heaven if not the infinite that journeys towards nothingness? What is nothingness if not a return, your return? What is the infinite if not a return?"[4] From denial to prayer? Or, in the restlessness of doubt, the faith of the believer and the prayer of one who would like to believe?

The Church of Love

"The Holy Spirit communicates Himself *to persons,* marking each member of the Church with the seal of a personal and unique relationship to the Trinity, becoming present in each person. How does this come about? That remains a mystery — the mystery of the self-emptying, of the κένωσις of the Holy Spirit's coming into the world. If in the κένωσις of the Son the person appeared to men while the Godhead remained hidden under the form of a servant, the Holy Spirit in His coming, while He manifests the common nature of the Trinity, leaves His own Person concealed beneath His Godhead. He remains unrevealed, hidden, so to speak, by the gift in order that this gift which He imparts may be fully ours, adapted to our persons."[5]

These words suggest the background against which to situate our reflection on the mystery of the church, which is the "icon" of the Trinity thanks to the Spirit who works in her as the invisible principle of her

3. *De Trinitate* 15.28.51: PL 42:1098.

4. A. Emo, *Le voci delle muse,* a cura di M. Donà e R. Gasparotti (Venezia: Marsilio, 1992), p. 75.

5. V. Lossky, *The Mystical Theology of the Eastern Church* (Crestwood, N.Y.: St. Vladimir's Seminary Press, 1976), p. 168.

unity in space ("communio") and time ("traditio"). This is an "icon" marked by humility and "kenosis": nonetheless, one that corresponds in the highest degree to that longing for unity which has emerged in the depths of human awareness after the collapse of the totalitarian ideologies, and in that loneliness which is often the postmodern condition.

Needing the Church

"A religious process of incalculable importance has begun — the Church is coming to life in the souls of men."[6] Written at the beginning of the 1920s, a dramatic and decisive time for the destinies of Europe and the world, these words sum up a way of reading those first troubled decades of the twentieth century, words that spoke with renewed awareness of a "need for the Church," to the point of describing that time as the "century of the Church."[7] The crisis provoked by the First World War had clearly demonstrated the limits of the modern confidence in the subject and in the absolute claims of reason, which both liberal-bourgeois and revolutionary culture had made their own. It was becoming evident that idealism's exaltation of subjectivity lacked the basic experience of reality: entrapped by ideology, "The man of this age . . . was not directly and strongly conscious of the reality of things, at bottom indeed not even of this own. . . . He lived . . . among concepts and mechanisms, among formulas and systems, which sought to represent and control objects, but which were not even coherent."[8] The ideologies were turning the very ideas of life in society and of community into a concern only for the masses: "There was indeed no community, merely a mechanical organization, and this in the religious sphere as in every other."[9] The church itself seemed to be responding to this trap set by modern reason by adopting an image of itself alternative to ideology's obsession with the masses, but for this reason exactly it was in fact of the same kind: "The Church appeared above all as a legal institution for religious purposes. There was

---

6. R. Guardini, *The Church and the Catholic and the Spirit of the Liturgy*, trans. Ada Lane (New York: Sheed & Ward), p. 11.

7. The expression is of O. Dibelius, *Das Jahrhundert der Kirche* (Berlin: Furche Verlag, 1926).

8. Guardini, *The Church and the Catholic*, pp. 13-14.

9. Guardini, *The Church and the Catholic*, p. 15.

no limit perception of the mystical element in her, everything in fact which lies behind her palpable aims and visible institutions, and is expressed by the concept of the kingdom of God, the mystical Body of Christ."[10]

Against this alienating ideology of the masses — whose effects lasted long, and indeed produced the most tragic fruits of the totalitarian systems that imposed themselves between the two world wars and beyond — there emerged the need for a return to real, concrete things, and thus to the infinite wealth and dignity of the individual: "Proofs are accumulating that people are willing to accept concrete reality as the one self-evident fact, and to base abstract truth upon it. . . . The concrete, in its boundless fulness, is being once more experienced, and the happiness of being able to venture oneself to it and enter into it."[11]

This development meant both a decisive rejection of the spell cast by idealism and the joyful rediscovery of the living community, made up of real, flesh-and-blood persons: "Modern idealism — against which the assaults of logic were so long delivered in vain, because the foundation of the system was not proof, but a dogmatic foundation of the mental attitude of the entire age — no longer needs to be refuted. The bottom has fallen out of it. Its spell is broken, and we ask ourselves how it is that we endured it so long. A great awakening to reality is in progress."[12]

Over against the domination of the subject, imposed with such force as to make the whole of reality somehow correspond to the ideal, there now reappears an attention for the presence of the other: in the widest sense, the church begins to reawaken in souls: "The reality of things, the reality of the soul and the reality of God, confront us with a new impressiveness. . . . In this religious relation our fellow men have a vital part. The religious community exists. Nor is it a collection of self-contained individuals, but the reality which comprehends individuals — the Church."[13]

We can understand, then, why Christians believe that the good news by which to respond to totalitarian violence and postmodern loneliness is

---

10. Guardini, *The Church and the Catholic*, p. 16.
11. Guardini, *The Church and the Catholic*, pp. 16-17.
12. Guardini, *The Church and the Catholic*, p. 17.
13. Guardini, *The Church and the Catholic*, pp. 223-23.

the communion of the church. The church is the space of the Other and of his real and liberating encounter with the person: this is the deep reason why the church is "reawakening in souls." Over against the obsession of the ideologies with the masses, the gospel of the church reminds us of the infinite dignity of every single person before God and before others, a dignity independent of the person's history and situation. Over against nihilism, the good news of the church affirms that it is really possible to encounter another person and to overcome loneliness through dialogue and solidarity, which are generated and sustained by the love that comes from God. In both cases, it is the good news of communion that sounds out as a plausible response to the deepest needs emerging from the contemporary crisis; and the church offers itself as the place where communion can be achieved here and now, thanks to the gift of God in Jesus Christ.

The Spirit: Creating Communion in Space and Time

"The grace of the Lord Jesus Christ, the love of God, and the communion of the Holy Spirit be with all of you" (2 Cor. 13:14): this formula, with its echoes of the early church at worship, brings together the confession of the Father's freely offered love in Jesus Christ and the communion wrought by the Holy Spirit. This communion entails both sharing in the life of the Spirit as well as in the fraternity that flows from there; or, better, it means fraternal communion is real if it is generated, nourished, and enlivened by the gift of the Spirit. We could say that grace, love, and communion, referred respectively to Christ, the Father, and the Spirit, are different aspects of the one sharing in the life of the Trinity, which generates the church of love willed by the Father, gathered by the grace of the Son, and manifested in history as communion in the Spirit: on earth, the church is the place of the love of the Three who are One.

The Fourth Gospel in particular perceives Christian fraternity as the direct consequence of the communion in God's life wrought by our encounter with Jesus in his Spirit: "The formula most frequently used by John to express the eschatological reality of the Church is the simple conjunction 'as' ('kathós'). This does not only establish a bond of likeness between Christ and his disciples, but also indicates that what exists in God must also be present in those who belong to him."[14] The loving communion that joins the Father to the Son and to human beings is at the same time the model and source of fraternal communion, which must unite the disciples among themselves: "The texts with 'kathós,' which affirm an ontological correspondence between the divine persons and the Christian community, lead to a command: 'This is my commandment, that you love one another as I have loved you' (John 15:12; cf. 13:34); or: 'That they may all be one . . . as we are one' (John 17:21-22)."[15] It is here that we notice the work of the Holy Spirit: communion, fruit of the grace of the Son and of the love of the Father, and made visible in mutual love, is "the communion of the Holy Spirit" (2 Cor. 13:14). It is thanks to the Spirit that the disciples give witness to the Master: "When the Advocate comes, whom I will send to you from the Father, the Spirit of truth who comes from the Father, he will testify on my behalf. You also are to testify . . ." (John 15:26f.). And witnessing to Jesus means fraternal communion: "By this everyone will know that you are my disciples, if you have love for one another" (John 13:35). The church of love, icon of the Trinity, is thus the church of the Spirit, who generates the communion of the disciples among themselves and with God, communicating himself to them through the Word of life, the sacraments of the faith, and the ministry of the shepherds who faithfully guard the Word proclaimed and celebrate the memorial of the Lord.

Communion in the Holy Spirit does not, however, only gather the believers at one particular time: it enfolds all times and makes it possible for succeeding generations to be united in faith and communication in the one Lord. The Spirit ensures that the mystery has this historical dimension, that it happens in time. Thanks to the Spirit, the original Christian experience of encountering the risen Jesus can always be lived anew in the worship and communion of God's pilgrim people in history, till all God's promises are fulfilled, and Christ returns in glory.

That this was Jesus' wish for his community — that he wanted the church his body, God's people of the new covenant in his blood, to con-

14. P. Le Fort, "Les structures de l'Eglise militante selon Saint Jean," *Etude d'ecclésiologie concrète appliqué au IVe évangile et aux épitres johanniques* (Genève: Labor et Fides, 1970), p. 172.
15. Le Fort, "Les structures de l'Eglise militante selon Saint Jean," p. 172.

tinue mystically in time — is indicated by the fact that from the beginning of his public ministry he set himself to gather the Israel of the last times. The drama of the chosen people's refusal to accept his message led Jesus to institute the twelve apostles as representatives of the twelve tribes, that is, of the church that will embrace all the families of the earth; and this church is called to draw all peoples towards the final Jerusalem, and to welcome them there. In the parables of the Kingdom as in the missionary discourses, Jesus makes clear his wish that the effects of what he is doing should reach the ends of the earth. After his resurrection, he explicitly entrusts the apostles with the task of making disciples of all nations, assuring them of his faithful presence and help till the end of time. Because salvation is for all, the memorial of Easter reconciliation must be celebrated without interruption till Christ's glorious return (cf. 1 Cor. 11:26).

It is the Holy Spirit who makes present in the here and now the Lord Jesus' saving presence, through the ministry of the pastors, heads of the families of eschatological Israel, and through the whole life of the people of the new covenant. The Acts of the Apostles provides a vivid account of this communion between the Spirit sent by Christ and the community gathered by them both to carry out in history the mission received from the risen Lord. "You will receive power when the Holy Spirit has come upon you; and you will be my witnesses in Jerusalem, in all Judea and Samaria, and to the ends of the earth" (Acts 1:8). The apostles and their companions are sent out on mission by the work of the Holy Spirit through the imposition of hands (cf., for example, Acts 13:3f.; 1 Tim. 4:14). When the church is called to reach solemn decisions, it is the Spirit who guides it: "It has seemed good to the Holy Spirit and to us . . ." (Acts 15:28). The church grows and journeys "in the fear of the Lord and the comfort of the Holy Spirit" (Acts 9:31). For the disciples the Spirit is the living memory of Jesus; he is the One who will teach them all things: "The Advocate, the Holy Spirit, whom the Father will send in my name, will teach you everything, and remind you of all that I have said to you" (John 14:26). The Spirit bears witness to Christ and makes the disciples able to do the same: "When the Spirit of truth comes, he will guide you into all the truth; for he will not speak on his own, but will speak whatever he hears, and he will declare to you the things that are to come" (John 16:13). And finally it is the Holy Spirit who is at work in the church's ministry, as the ever new source of forgiveness and life: "Receive the Holy Spirit. If you forgive the sins of any, they are forgiven them; if you retain the sins of any, they are retained" (20:22).

This permanent presence of Christ in his people, wrought by the Holy Spirit through the Word and the sacraments of the church, is what theology calls the "apostolic tradition." It is not simply what apostles received at the beginning and then passed on, but the active presence of the crucified and risen Lord in the whole history of the community gathered by him. Tradition — rightly distinguished from traditions, both particular and contingent — is communion with the Holy Spirit as he is present in time, the unity — made possible by him — between the experience of the apostolic faith, as lived in the first community of disciples, and the church's present experience of Christ. Tradition is the living gospel, proclaimed by the apostles in its completeness, proceeding from the fullness of their unique and unrepeatable experience, inasmuch as this gospel finds expression among believers — in time and space — under the influence of the Holy Spirit who gives life. Tradition is the history of the Spirit at work in the history of the church, as he makes it possible for the church day by day to receive the Word and the silence of God; it is the place where we pass from the letter to the Spirit of the scriptures.

This is exactly why Tradition is fully "apostolic": established as heads of the eschatological Israel, the twelve continue the mission begun by the Lord, and pass on faithfully through their successors the gift received, the good news of the Kingdom which has come to human beings in Jesus Christ. The community of the disciples, thus born, recognizes itself as founded on the witness of those who first encountered the Lord, guided and instructed by them and by as many as they associated with themselves in the ministry of the Word and communion, committed to transmitting to others the living presence of the Lord in the Spirit. History thus becomes part of faith: "At the beginning — writes a very ancient witness — (the apostles) affirmed the faith in Jesus Christ and established Churches in Judea. Immediately afterwards, they spread throughout the world and announced the same doctrine and the same faith to the nations and then founded Churches in every city. From these, the other churches took the beginnings of their faith and the seeds of doctrine, and they continually draw on these in order to be truly Churches. In this way also they are considered apostolic as being descendants of the Churches of the Apostles."[16] Thanks to this continuity of the faith in time and space, the church is one, holy, catholic, and apostolic: people of God united in the sanctifying Spirit, in the universality and in the fullness of communion which is based on the foundation of the apostles and which lives from the faith transmitted by the apostolic tradition. Precisely thus the church is the good news against loneliness, the community arising from above in which may be overcome the imprisonment of the subject enclosed in himself, incapable of communicating and loving. In this sense, one is not a Christian outside the church: the disciple of Christ is either in the church, living of it and for it, or he is not. On the seas of history, he will never be a solitary navigator, but always someone who remains and lives with faith and love in the ship of Peter, to reach in it and with it all the shores towards which the wind of the Spirit pushes the sails of the one ship of the Lord. . . .

Faith and History

The Trinity and the Human Community

For many, the Trinity is little more than an abstract heavenly theorem with no relevance at all for real life. It was Karl Rahner who observed: "We must be willing to admit that, should the doctrine of the Trinity have to be dropped as false, the major part of religious literature could well remain virtually unchanged. . . . One has the feeling that, for the catechism of head and heart (as contrasted with the printed catechism), the Christian's idea of the incarnation would not have to change at all if there were no Trinity."[17]

And yet, for Christians everything is done in the name of the Trinity and to their glory: the redeemed existence is like a living "Amen" to the twofold Trinitarian confession: the first, at baptism — "In the name of the Father and of the Son and of the Holy Spirit" — on which is founded the identity of the disciples; the second, in praise — "Glory be to the Father and to the Son and to the Holy Spirit" — in which their vocation and mission is expressed. To overcome "the exile of the Trinity" is, therefore,

---

16. Tertullian, *De praescriptione haereticorum* (circa 200), 20; PL 2.32.

17. K. Rahner, *The Trinity,* trans. J. Donceel (New York: Crossroad, 1997), pp. 10-11.

an essential and urgent challenge. In particular, we have to rediscover the fruitful link between the Trinity and the real history of human beings. Twentieth-century European theology essayed such a reflection, not without some risks and debatable conclusions.

In debate with Carl Schmitt's "political theology," which argued that the theological concepts of a given time are in fact instruments wielded by the dominant political and social structures,[18] Erik Petersen maintained that though this may be the case with monotheism, it is not so with the Trinity.[19] Petersen insisted that, while monotheism may have provided a theological underpinning for keeping the empire together, the orthodox doctrine of the Trinity had instead seriously threatened the political theology of the Roman empire. This explains, according to him, how, on the one hand, there was at first an urgent political concern to push the emperors into the Arian camp, and how, on the other, the Arians were destined to become the theologians of the Byzantine court. Only the Trinitarian faith, he insists, guaranteed the necessary critical freedom vis-à-vis the dominant political power.

While recognizing the importance of Petersen's thesis for the times when he expounded it, dominated as they were by the Nazi barbarities, it is not difficult to note how monotheism has often been critical, or even subversive, of political power: it is enough to think of the biblical prophets! The simple deduction of a political attitude from Trinitarian faith does not stand: the theological truth is more complex than the ways in which it may be manipulated!

This is not sufficient reason, though, to give up every idea of a political theology founded on the confession of the Trinity: that this is the case is shown by how the problem continues to present itself. Among the various positions on the subject that have emerged in the European context we can identify two main approaches. On the one hand, there is a prevalently critical political theology, of which Johannes Baptist Metz's writings are an example;[20] Metz points to the "eschatological reserve" contained in Christian revelation as the basis for a permanently dialectical

18. C. Schmitt, *Politische Theologie. Vier Kapitel zur Lehre von der Souveränität* (1922; München, 1951), pp. 45-147.

19. E. Petersen, *Der Monotheismus als politisches Problem* (Leipzig, 1935).

20. Cf. J. B. Metz, "Chiesa e mondo alla luce di una teologia politica," in *Sulla teologia del mondo* (Brescia: Queriniana, 1969), pp. 105-23. Cf. also by the same author *La fede nella storia e nella società* (Brescia: Queriniana, 1978).

relationship with each historical moment. On the other hand is a somewhat more positive approach, exemplified by the work of Jürgen Moltmann,[21] who succeeds in formulating a true and proper Trinitarian social doctrine, almost providing a "third way" beyond personalism and socialism, in the direction of what we might call social personalism or personal socialism. Such a "political theology," however, deduced from the Trinitarian model, runs the risk, first, of staying rather vague and thus failing to offer truly practical guidelines and, second, of attributing sacred power to a political formula, and so of laying itself open to manipulation. So we need to look in other directions, beginning from the very basis of the relationship between creature and Creator.

Witnesses of the Trinity at the Service of Reconciliation

From what has been said so far there emerges a list of priorities, a kind of "ten commandments" to be lived in the service of reconciliation between individuals and peoples in the postmodern world, challenging us to think and make choices in our historical situation, not only as individual believers, but also as the church and in the human community at the cultural, religious, and political levels. This list points to an urgent moral and spiritual program in which the Trinity is seen as a source of contemporary inspiration for the community of peoples in relation, first, to human beings as they go out of themselves (their exodus), second, to God's coming in history and, third, to the encounter with God in the hearts of men and women called to be builders of justice and peace.

In the first place, then, the provisional nature of the human condition has to be accepted and lived as such: this means that every human being, and especially every individual believer and the church, is called to live in a continual exodus from self towards the other. *Do not shut yourself up in yourself, do not become a prisoner of your own anxieties and defensiveness!* This call is urgent in order for us to open ourselves to listen to and welcome the others who meet us both in and outside of our own community, with their challenges, peculiarities, needs, and differences.

---

21. Cf. J. Moltmann, *The Trinity and the Kingdom: The Doctrine of God,* trans. Margaret Kohl (San Francisco: Harper & Row, 1981), especially pp. 191ff.: "Criticism of Political and Clerical Monotheism."

Here arises a second call, underscoring the urgent need to go beyond not only the comfortable ghetto of the individual, but also the potential ghetto of our own ethnic, cultural, or religious group: *"Do not shut yourself up in a cozy sense of belonging, or in the selfish interests of your group!"* The call is to tear down the walls of every possible sense of conflict that makes an enemy of whatever is different, feeding on the suspicion and hostility that exist between cultures and ethnic groups, between rich and poor, between religions and nations: the dynamic movement of the Trinity is a model for all of us to move out of our ghettos and to accept others, and it is the foundation of a fraternity that is at one and the same time both truly universal and practical.

These two precepts, though, which aim at preventing individuals and communities from shutting themselves up in themselves, need to be linked at once to a positive call to be open to recognize and welcome others: inasmuch as human beings are created to go beyond themselves towards ultimate Mystery, they are also called to listen to the transcendent and sovereign Other who comes to meet them in the signs of creation and the history of salvation. We could put it thus: *"Open yourself to the holy Mystery, enfolding you and all that lives, and help the seeker for that Mystery that is within you, and in every restless heart, to recognize the signs of Mystery's presence in life and history!"* In the "global village" which our planet has become, this appeal underlines the urgent need to propose the centrality of the question of God and of the last things with fresh vigor, going beyond an aridly theoretical approach and the resistance rooted in the totalitarian claims of ideological reason and nihilistic resignation.

This also underlines, though, how urgent it is to be open to the value of every "otherness" that comes to meet and visit us as individuals and communities, understanding such difference not as competition or threat, but promise and gift: *"Respect others in their difference from you, and be ready to welcome the gift and enrichment they represent for you and your community!"* Individuals and communities are called to give up any idea of simply disposing of others according to the logic of their own interest, and to reject any recourse to violence in whatever form, whether physical or psychological, in order rather to measure themselves against the positive potential of meeting others, no matter what may be the real difficulties involved. We can thus perceive how the experience of reconciliation between persons requires an openness to the real coming among us of the Other: this is the place of faith, by which the human heart opens itself to the gift of God and lets itself be molded by him.

Regarding God's coming, therefore, there is above all the call to welcome the gift of faith, which the believer cannot but offer to all, even and especially in this postmodern age: *"In the obedience of faith, welcome the gift of God offered in Jesus Christ. Be not unbelieving, but believe!"* The uniqueness of Jesus Christ is constitutive of Christian identity: without it there is no faith, no community of salvation, no passion and sense of urgency in mission. European modernity has made this a matter of debate: in the name of the universal claim to truth made by adult reason, there has been the attempt to set the incontestable power of rational truths against the weakness and fragility of truths rooted in facts or events. Among these latter must be numbered Christian truth, rooted in the story of the prophet from Galilee.

Yet the crisis of this rationalistic understanding of truth is evident in the appalling violence produced by the ideologies; and this crisis has led to a rediscovery of the singularity of the true, the "universale concretum et personale," which Christian revelation confesses in Jesus Christ. In this postmodern age, Christians are called to give an account of their hope in a convincing and persevering way, with gentleness and respect towards all (cf. 1 Peter 3:15), but also in the awareness that there may be no delay in proclaiming the good news to this age as it emerges from the intoxication of ideological reason. The more individual Christians nourish themselves with the spirit of the Beatitudes, the more they give the first place to faith in Jesus Christ, the more will they recognize themselves as called to serve the people of the world, marked as these are by crisis, with their witness to and proclamation of the gospel. This energy, flowing from the love of Christ, can be expressed in this appeal, directed to the church and to individual believers: *"Live your faith in such a way as to show the strength and beauty of the reconciliation given in Christ, and so as to announce it in season and out of season — good news for every human being and for the whole human being, as well as for the entire community of the peoples of the earth!"*

Finally, in relation to the encounter between exodus and advent, celebrated and lived out in faith in Jesus Christ, the source of new life for believers and for all, it is possible to identify four basic points that translate the commitment to the service of reconciliation lived in the light of the Trinity into the practicalities of personal and community relationships.

First, there can be no true acceptance of God's love that is not expressed in an ethic of solidarity, that recognizes the needs of others, especially the weakest and poorest, as rights against which to measure oneself and for which to commit oneself. *"Live in solidarity with others, recognizing in their need and weakness their right to your commitment and to the commitment of the church and civil society!"* For a humanity ever more dramatically scarred by tensions between ethnic groups and nations, in the context of growing economic globalization, with the increasing tendency to undermine any gains in social justice in the name of economy and profit, this appeal for solidarity is more urgent than ever. We need to ensure that the first place is given to the person over the crude logic of the market and the absolute value of profit; and this can be done in an especially convincing way if our inspiration is God's plan for authentic human growth as this is revealed in Jesus Christ and proclaimed by the church.

Second, for such action inspired by solidarity to be credible, believers must show by deeds their capacity for mutual acceptance and dialogue both within the church and between the denominations, as well as in interreligious dialogue. This could be summed up in this way: *"Live with a passion for the unity of the body of Christ, committing yourself to the search for full communion with all believers in him, and accept religious diversity with respect, promoting dialogue and collaboration with all believers in God, whatever faith they belong to!"* There is a need for practical experiences of dialogue and cooperation, which can become laboratories in which to learn how to overcome fundamentalism and to create opportunities for mutual knowledge and common witness in truth and charity.

The spirit of solidarity and of civil and religious dialogue will not, however, fully express the gift of reconciliation if it is not able at the same time to open itself to the dimensions of the whole world. In a world that becomes ever more a "global village," where economic, social, and political dependence between peoples and continents is ever more marked, it is no longer admissible for people to deny their part of responsibility for building a new and more just international economic order and a more correct relationship between human beings and the whole of creation. In these relationships on a global scale it is urgent that we move from conflict to fraternity, to the achievement of peaceful coexistence between peoples, especially excluding those forms of poverty that are not endemic, but which are the result of economic inequality that produces the exclusion and abject poverty of such a large portion of humanity.

Third, to this economic, social, and political commitment there must be added a commitment to the environment, which above all bears the mark of the creating Trinity, so that an ecological awareness and the resulting action to safeguard creation inspire the behavior both of individuals and groups, in the awareness that the balanced and healthy survival of the ecosystem is entrusted to the care of each and all and concerns each human person and community. This cluster of concerns could be summed up thus: *"Be aware of your responsibilities for the whole human family and for that great home which is the world, and act so as to favor growth in the quality of life for all in justice and in respect for creation!"*

Finally, the new life that flows from the gift of the revelation of the Trinity is open to the fulfillment of God's promises at the time when Christ will hand everything over to the Father, and God will be all in all (cf. 1 Cor. 15:28). The movement towards complete eschatological reconciliation calls for a continuous reform of positions already attained, a need for incessant conversion and renewal to draw the future of God ever more into the human present. This means doing deeds that anticipate the future, full of prophetic meaning on the basis of the gift already offered to human beings in Christ; the new life of those who have let themselves be reconciled to God finds its program in the Beatitudes, which are at once the fruit of God's gift and a demanding experience that prefigures the fulfillment of his promise.

The nonviolence of the peaceful is the style proper to those who — faced with conflict — believe in the "impossible possibility" of God and of his love for women and men. Especially in Europe, where the crisis of the great ideological models produced by the modern age appears deepest, and where the temptation to nihilistic resignation and irresponsible escapisms seems strongest, Christians must be ready to walk the paths of conversion, renewal, and service in charity. This complex of challenges could be expressed thus: *"Live in constant conversion and renewal and be open to God's surprises; have the courage to pay the supreme price so that the promised reconciliation may take shape in the lives of human beings!"*

The "ten commandments" thus essayed are at once a challenge and a promise for whoever has believed in the gospel of the Trinity and experienced the power of the reconciliation which that gospel offers, as a gift of God and source of new life. For Christians, such a gospel constitutes a program aimed at achieving the interaction of faith and life at the beginning of the third millennium. No believer can legitimately ignore this challenge. To the disciples of the risen Lord — both as individuals and as communities — there falls the task of accepting it and proposing it to others with the conviction of words and of life.

Towards the Beauty of God

Our modern age is characterized in its most various expressions by the desire for wholeness: emancipation, the inspiring soul of the Enlightenment project, is impatient with every limitation. Whether the impatient protagonist be the subjective spirit, understood in modern idealism as a phenomenon of the absolute Spirit, or whether a class or historical movement as in the revolutionary version, the final result is just the same: the "other" is absorbed, the subject (personal or collective) reigns supreme, and there is no room left for difference. The presumptuous spirit of emancipated reason thus flows inevitably into totalitarianism, which has no time for the unexpected, the singular, the new; and, wielded by one or other historical system, this spirit turns violent.

The "dialectic of the Enlightenment" notes instead the historical failure of the great modern ideological "narratives," and calls for a critical overturning of their claim to totality. It insists on the renewed significance of difference, considered able to break apart the tight, all-encompassing circle of adult reason. Against totalitarianism's proud boasts, there is a new awareness of the need for a return to the humble, the concrete. The unrepeatable dignity of every fragment, with all its lights and shadows, emerges with new vigor; the provisional, the singular, the not entirely understood, all acquire new importance.

At the same time, in reaction and response to the loneliness provoked by nihilism, the urgent need is felt of rediscovering a shared horizon: the transcendence of the true and its unifying power re-emerge as the non-ideological Whole that appears in the fragment and redeems it. This Whole, present in the fragment, is beauty: in its deepest sense, for the believer it is the beauty revealed in the "beautiful Shepherd" (John 10:11), who makes us beautiful (cf. Matt. 5:16).

Of this beauty the believer is offered a rich, real foretaste in a creature, Mary, the "all beautiful," icon of the whole Christian mystery. This beauty is simultaneously mortal and salvific, because it lays bare the shortsightedness of all that passes and throws light on our yearning for that which does not pass. Our journey as pilgrims of faith in time tends towards this beauty, till we reach the fulfillment of God's promises, when he will be all in all, and the whole world will be his beauty's home.

The Beautiful Woman

"'Mother of God': the name alone contains the whole mystery of the work of Incarnation":[1] these words of St. John Damascene — the "seal of the Fathers" as the Eastern church loves to call him — express an enduring Christian conviction about Mary. Inasmuch as the Virgin Mother is totally relative to the mystery of the incarnate Word, she is a compendium of the gospel and a singular, flesh-and-blood expression of the church's faith. Indeed, "the deep structure of the mystery of Mary is the same as that of the Covenant, but viewed from the point of view of us human beings, whom Mary represents."[2] When faith tells of her, it perceives how in her the mysteries are intimately interwoven in the unity of God.

The scriptures themselves are the first to witness to this, when, regarding her, they affirm what we can call a law of wholeness: on the one hand, it is evident that we cannot speak of her except in relation to her Son, and to all the deeds of revelation and of salvation achieved in him; on the other, the biblical texts are so powerfully expressive in the way they speak of the Mother's relationship with the Son that she reverberates with everything accomplished in him. So we can say that Mary's story is "the sum of the world's story, a theology of the world in one word"; that she is "living dogma, the truth about the fulfilled creature."[3] Mary is the woman, icon of Mystery.

1. St. John Damascene, *De fide orthodoxa* 3.12; PG 94:1029C.

2. I. de la Potterie, *Maria nel mistero dell'alleanza* (Genova: Marietti, 1988), p. 279.

3. P. Evdokimov, *La donna e la salvezza del mondo* (Milano: Jaca Book, 1980), pp. 54 and 216.

Mary, Woman, Icon of Mystery

To speak of Mary as woman underlines, in the first place, the flesh-and-blood, historical reality of this girl of the house of Israel, who was granted the extraordinary experience of becoming the mother of the Messiah. Certainly, it is impossible in the Gospels to unearth a biography of Mary, just as it is to reconstruct a biography of Jesus. The Gospels witness to Easter: with eyes lit by the experience of meeting the Risen One, they reread only those aspects and moments of the pre-Easter events that are of special significance for the faith.

All the same, several factors gives us the confidence to paint a historically reliable, if very spare, portrait of Mary: the many sources that speak of her; the fact that some of the basic statements concerning her cannot be simply explained by reference to the cultural and historical context of her time (first among these, the idea of the virginal conception); and the criterion of the continuity and internal harmony of the gospel message.

The great things that befell her must thus not cause us to forget the lowliness of her background, the ordinariness of her work in the family at Nazareth, the darkness of faith in which she walked, the way she was molded by her environment, the fact that she had personal experience of the different ways of being a woman, as virgin, mother, and spouse. Mary is no myth, nor is she an abstraction, as is shown by the deeply Hebrew traits of her personality as a woman, who knew how to live the faith and messianic hope of her people to the highest degree, as she experienced in herself both their fulfillment and their new beginning in an entirely unheard-of and amazing way.

This particular woman was the place where God came into the flesh of the world, but without her losing any of her womanhood. Mary is not merely one case of the universal; she is rather the "Virgo singularis," a historically unique and unrepeatable woman, a person of real, intense femininity, whom the Eternal chose for the revelation of the Mystery: and it is from his Son — the concrete universal, norm, and archetype of the human — that the Virgin Mary receives her own specific and singular share in the universality of the divine plan, "blessed among women" as is "blessed the fruit of her womb" (Luke 1:42).

We are thus not concerned here with developing any so-called "ontology of the feminine," starting from Mary, Virgin-Mother-Spouse. The risks of such abstract research into the "eternal feminine"[4] have been jus-tifiably denounced. It is rather a matter of inquiring into some aspects of the mystery enfolded in every woman, and thus reciprocally in every man, beginning from the absolutely singular case, the woman "Virgin Mary, daughter of her Son." The universal significance of Mary, then, stands or falls on her singularity as a flesh-and-blood woman: the more her uniqueness as a woman is understood, the more her value as an ar-chetype for the feminine dimension of the human being can be per-ceived, and the more the mystery in her can be appreciated.

It is this interplay between visible reality and invisible depth that leads us to speak of Mary as an icon. She is an icon because there is in her the double movement of which every icon tends to speak, descent and as-cent, an anthropology of God and a theology of the human person. In her there shines the fact that she was chosen by the Eternal God and her free assent of faith in him. As "the icon is the vision of things not seen,"[5] so the Virgin Mary offers herself to the gaze of faith as the place of the divine Presence, the ark of the covenant, covered by the shadow of the Holy Spirit (cf. Luke 1:35 and 39-45, 56), the holy dwelling of the Word of life among humankind. And as an icon needs color and form to proclaim and give life to what the Bible says in words,[6] so the Mother of the Lord bears the mystery in the reality of who she actually is. To look at Mary the "icon" means, then, to examine the biblical data about her with eyes that are ready to sound the divine depths communicated in the text, in just the way the uninterrupted believing tradition of the church has read them from the very beginning. Meditating on Mary in the scriptures, we are enabled to reread the scriptures in Mary, to grasp in what the Bible says about the Mother of the Lord the whole realization of the covenant narrated in a fragment.

Mary is the woman who is the icon of Mystery, of God's plan of sal-vation, hidden in time, but now revealed in Jesus Christ, glory concealed under the signs of history.[7] This mystery is at one and the same time the visible events in which it is fulfilled, and the invisible depth of the divine

4. The expression "eternal feminine" ("das Ewigweibliche") is found at the end of Goethe's *Faust* (Part II, Act V, 12110) and has met with extraordinary success.

5. P. Evdokimov, *La donna e la salvezza del mondo*, p. 133. Cf. by the same author, *Teologia della bellezza. L'arte dell'icona*, 3rd ed. (Roma: Paoline, 1982).

6. Cf. IV Council of Constantinople (879): *DS* 654.

7. Cf. Rom. 16:25; 1 Cor. 2:7f.; Eph. 1:9; 3:3; 6:19; Col. 1:25-27; 1 Tim. 3:16.

work achieved in them. In this way, the mystery embraces the truth about God and the truth about human beings, created and redeemed by Christ: and this truth offers itself in him, who is in person "the way, the truth, and the life" (John 14:6). Mary is entirely relative to him, to his mystery as incarnate Word: already in the annunciation, which is a deeply meaningful foretaste of Easter, the Trinity is revealed as the adorable womb that receives the holy Virgin, and at the same time Mary is presented as the womb of God.[8] Enfolded in the Father's plan, Mary will be covered by the shadow of the Spirit who will make of her the mother of the eternal Son made flesh.

Between Mary and the Trinity is thus established a relationship of unique depth: she is "the sanctuary and the repose of the most holy Trinity,"[9] the Trinity's image or icon. In the flesh-and-blood experience of Mary the woman, we can thus discern the various dimensions of redeemed existence as a share in the Trinitarian life and a yearning for the Trinity's glory to be fulfilled. The All offers himself in the fragment of her who, precisely because of this, we call "tota pulchra," the beautiful woman, with a beauty that is without spot or wrinkle.

The All in a Fragment of History

The three aspects of Mary's life on earth are linked to the three divine Persons: as Virgin, she stands before the Father in pure receptivity, and offers herself as an icon of him who in eternity is pure receiving, the Generated, the Beloved, the eternal Son, the Word come forth from silence. As Mother of the Incarnate Word, Mary relates to the Father in the unconditional giving, which is the source of life-giving love, and so she is the motherly icon of him who has loved since before time began, the Generating One, eternal Lover, the Father, source and end of silence. As ark of the covenant by which heaven is married to earth, the Spouse in whom the Eternal One unites history to himself and fills it with his gift,

---

8. It is a scene of Trinitarian significance: "Its narrative structure reveals for the first time in an absolutely clear way the Trinity of God": H. Urs von Balthasar, "Maria nella dottrina e nel culto della Chiesa," in J. Ratzinger and H. Urs von Balthasar, *Maria Chiesa nascente* (Roma: Paoline, 1981), pp. 48f.

9. St. Louis M. Grignon de Montfort, *Trattato della vera devozione alla Santa Vergine*, in *Opere* (Roma: Edizioni Monfortane, 1990), p. 1, n. 5.

Mary relates to the communion between Father and Son, and between them and the world, and so is the icon of the Holy Spirit, place of the eternal betrothal, bond of infinite love and permanent openness of the living God to the history of human beings. In the Virgin Mother, then, there is the reflection of the very mystery of the divine relationships: in the unity of her person she bears the very imprint of the Triune God.

This Trinitarian communion is also reflected in the mystery of the church: also an icon of the Trinity, the church finds in the adorable mystery of the Three its origin, model, and home. The church comes from the Trinity, who give it life by the wonderful initiative of the Father and the missions of the Son and Spirit; and the church journeys towards the Trinity, living in its own way that life of Trinitarian movement in which the diversity of gifts and forms of service are rooted in the unity of the Spirit, to show forth the Trinity in the dialogue of communion.

Both icons of the Trinity in this way, the relationship between Mary and the Trinity has to be one of symbolic identity, as Christian faith has perceived from the beginning: Mary the woman is the church, daughter of Zion in the age of entirely unexpected messianic fulfillment. "The links between Our Lady and the Church are not only numerous and close; they are essential, woven from within. . . . In the Church's tradition the same biblical symbols are applied, either in turn or simultaneously, with one and the same ever increasing profusion, to the Church and Our Lady":[10] new Eve, Paradise, ladder of Jacob, Ark of the Covenant. . . .

In the Mother of the Lord the church contemplates her own mystery, not only because she finds there the model of virginal faith, maternal charity, and wedded covenant, to all of which she is called, but also because she recognizes in Mary her own archetype, the ideal of what the church must be, temple of the Spirit, mother of children generated in the Son, and the Body of him born in flesh from the Virgin. Thus, if on the one hand the life of Mary is "substance and revelation of the mystery of the Church," on the other "truly the Church is the Mary of universal history."[11] Mary, the Virgin-Mother-Spouse, icon of the mystery of God, is then analogously icon of the mystery of the church.

Mary is also simply the human creature before God: a real, individual

---

10. H. de Lubac, *The Splendor of the Church,* trans. Michael Mason (San Francisco: Ignatius, 1986), pp. 317-18.

11. H. Rahner, *Maria e la Chiesa* (Milano: Paoline, 1974), pp. 79 and 68.

creature, a unique and unrepeatable woman, partner in a dialogue with the Eternal, a dialogue with all the characteristics of creation and redemption. The Spirit overshadows her, recalling the first creation, when "the spirit of God swept over the face of the waters" (Gen. 1:2); in her we are reminded of the first woman (cf. Gen. 3:15, and the use of the term "woman" for Mary in the Fourth Gospel); she is the servant of the Lord, blessed because she "believed that there would be a fulfillment of what was spoken to her by the Lord" (Luke 1:45); she is the humble one, towards whom the Lord has turned his face, doing great things in her (cf. Luke 1:48ff.).

In Mary's "yes" is reflected all the greatness of God's creating work: the dignity of the creature, enabled to give free assent to the loving designs of the Eternal One, and so become in some fashion a coworker with God. The Lord, who chooses Mary and receives her consent, does not compete with human beings; the Eternal One, moved only by freely given love, has created us without us, but because of the very same love he will not save us without our free consent. In the Virgin Mary, we might say, the anthropology of God corresponds to the theology of the human being: the descending movement calls forth a movement of ascent. Freely, God chooses and calls; in Mary, the human being, chosen and called, responds in freedom and by freely given assent.

This anthropology of God — revealed in the annunciation — makes clear what was planned by the Eternal One since the world's first morning; it bears within it the imprint of the life of the Trinitarian God. The Virgin, receptive in a way that reflects the receptivity of the Son, is the believer: in faith she listens, accepts, and consents. The Mother, generous in a way that reflects the superabundant generosity of the Father, generates life: in charity she gives, offers, shares. The Spouse, accepting a new betrothal by the love of the Spirit, is the creature rich in hope: she knows how to unite the human present to the future promised by God.

Faith, love, and hope are the reflection in Mary of the depth of her assent to the Trinity's initiative and to the way this initiative seals her forever. As she believes, hopes, and loves, the Virgin Mother is as an icon of the human being desired by God. In her, too, we learn to see that all human beings are in fact called to be icons of the Trinity, who created and redeemed us, and to whose work of salvation we are called to offer our free, generously given consent. In the fragment that is Mary there shines out the beauty of the whole plan of God for his creatures.

All this is achieved in Mary without diminishing the reality of her particular, individual womanhood, but rather precisely through this: what is manifested in her is not some sort of abstract humanity, but feminine humanity in the flesh-and-blood reality of her being Virgin-Mother-Spouse. In her, creature before the Creator and redeemed human being before her Lord, humanity appears in its original, its necessary, completeness, with its two reciprocal poles: feminine and masculine. Here too the law of completeness is at work: the polarity sends us back to the whole. "The woman is another 'I' in shared humanity. . . . In the 'unity of the two' man and woman are called from the beginning not only to exist 'one beside the other' or 'together,' but also reciprocally, 'one for the other.'"[12] The creation of Adam (a collective term in Hebrew) is the creation of the original human being as man-woman, in the completeness of the beginning that sends us forward to the completeness of the end, where "there is no longer male and female; for you are all one in Christ Jesus" (Gal. 3:28). "In the Lord woman is not independent of man or man independent of woman. For just as woman came from man, so man comes through woman; but all things come from God" (1 Cor. 11:11ff.).

Because of how uniquely close Mary is to the new and perfect man, Jesus, she reflects in herself, in her true and full femininity, the totality of the human in its original and final unity: her whole life-story — from the immaculate conception to her bodily assumption in the glory of God — fully reveals God's plan for human beings. In her the feminine is not an alternative, or in opposition, to the masculine; on the contrary, the feminine reveals the depths of the masculine precisely in its identity as feminine and in the reciprocity by which it lives and to which it calls. Entirely relative to Christ, Mary lives in this completeness, integrating her femininity into the fullness of the new humanity: thus, to contemplate her in her truth as a woman means to rediscover in her the femininity of a humanity which is complete, the feminine revealing the masculine by way of reciprocity and integration, and which allows the characteristics of the new creature in the Lord to shine forth.

As Virgin, Mary was receptive in a fruitful and anything but passive way; as Mother, she lived with a pure generosity, formed in her by the freely given love of the Father which she shares with human beings; as Spouse, she lives the reciprocity of the covenant in a way that is both lib-

---

12. John Paul II, Apostolic Letter *Mulieris dignitatem* (August 15, 1988), nos. 6 and 7.

erating and a foretaste of what is still to come. All this reveals not only the femininity of the woman, but also what is feminine in the human, those dimensions of life, that is, which all human beings must take to themselves to be completely fulfilled according to God's plan.

Model and Mother, Mary helps each of Jesus' disciples to fulfill the project of the Eternal One, which was manifested in her, not in the solitude of a spirit shut in on itself, but in the communion of fruitful relationships which she lived and lives with each of the divine Persons, in the Trinity and in the church. Her beauty calls forth and aids our own: in both there is a share in the infinite beauty of God.

Mortal, Saving Beauty

Beauty: Splendid Generosity

Beauty is an event: it happens when the Whole, the All, offers itself to us in the fragment, when the Infinite makes itself little. Classically, beauty is "formosus": it happens when the different parts of what we behold come together in harmonious proportion, and remind us of "the heavenly numbers" and their own, celestial harmony. And beauty is "speciosus"; it shines out: this happens when the fragment we contemplate seems to capture the Whole, to be the place where the Whole breaks through to us with the wound and gift of love. Here the Greek soul and Christianity's new vision meet. Here Christianity takes Athena to itself and then betrays her, because — though Christianity, too, longs to contemplate the Whole in the fragment — it proclaims that beauty happened once and for all in a garden outside the walls of Jerusalem.

The cross of beauty is raised on the hill of Calvary. In this world, the Word says who he is by emptying and "abbreviating" himself. Quite freely, in no way coerced by the Infinitely Great, he lets himself be contained in the infinitely small, so that eternal splendor may come and offer itself in the midst of the world's night. This "ecstasy of God," when he goes out from himself, is the mightiest conceivable call for us to live our own "ecstasy from the world," to "go beyond" all things, towards the mystery that saves us by its beauty, in the way made possible when the Word Incarnate poured himself out for love, on the cross. Christ, the crucified God, is the place where beauty happens: in his self-emptying, eternity is present in time, the All who is God is present in the fragment of Christ's human form (cf. Phil. 2:6ff.). It is the cross that reveals the beauty that saves.

"Two flutes," explains Augustine, "play different tunes, but the same Spirit breathes through them both. The first: 'You are the most handsome of men' (Ps. 45:2); and the second: 'He had no form or majesty that we should look at him' (Isa. 53:2). The two flutes are played by one and the same Spirit: so they play in harmony. Do not fail to listen to them, but try to understand them. Let us ask the apostle Paul to explain the perfect harmony between the two flutes. Let the first play: 'the most handsome of men,' 'though he was in the form of God, he did not regard equality with God as something to be grasped' (Phil. 2:6). This is how the beauty of the sons of men is surpassed. Let the second play: 'that we should look at him,' he who 'emptied himself, taking the form of a slave, being born in human likeness' (Phil. 2:7). 'He had no form or majesty' so that he might give you beauty and form. What beauty? What form? The love of charity, so that you may run in love and love with the energy of one who runs. . . . Look to him through whom you have been made beautiful."[13] It is the love with which he has loved us that transfigures the "man of suffering and acquainted with infirmity . . . from whom others hide their faces" (Isa. 53:3) into "the most handsome of men": crucified love is the beauty that saves. The "beautiful shepherd," who dies abandoned on the cross, is the savior of the world!

Beauty has, thus, its tragic aspect: its kiss is mortal. The Whole that offers itself in the fragment shows how finite the fragment really is: Beauty lays bare the fragility of the beautiful. Beauty is like death, threatening us as it approaches: the experience of beauty is mixed with sadness. Beauty reminds us dwellers in time that we inhabit no mighty fortress: our home lies shrouded in the silence of nothingness. And so beauty can make us anxious: our hearts, suspended over the abyss of the silences of death, with beauty standing over us, become restless about their destiny.

Beauty troubles us: we flee it as we flee death. We transform it into entertainment, reduced to a good to be consumed: perhaps thus, we think, we may elude the pain of its challenge, and not have to think any more; perhaps thus we can escape the demanding passion for truth, and

13. St. Augustine, *In Io. Ep.* 9.9; PL 35:2051.

throw ourselves into enjoying what may be had here and now, and consumed at once. In the great marketplace of the "global village," the signs of beauty's presence seem to be disappearing. Advertising's masks seem to be triumphing on all fronts over respect for the tragic seriousness and vulnerable advent of ultimate truth and beauty. The "eclipse of beauty," its reduction to what is merely passing, seems to say that the fragile fragment does not have the strength to bear the weight of the Whole within it. . . .

And yet, if the "beautiful shepherd" (John 10:11) gave himself up to death for us, if in the fragment of the cross he opened the way for us to risen life, then in him, too, we may rediscover the Beauty that is beyond shipwreck. In him, as he opens us towards the ultimate horizon of all things, we are given to know the destiny of the fragment that was home to the Eternal. In the abandonment of the cross, the Whole revealed and hid itself, spoke and was silent about itself. And there it showed that the Whole does not only reveal how fragile the fragment is, but is also the horizon that defends its dignity. Christ, crucified beauty in dereliction, both gathers in himself the whole enigma of our human condition, and watches over the future intended for us and the world.

This is what is revealed to the eyes of faith by the death of the Son of God in the dark hours of Good Friday and in his rising to life. It is in this death and resurrection of the humble One that beauty goes beyond itself, and helps us dwellers in time to pass beyond death and to redeem the fragment. Good Friday and Easter Sunday: God goes out from himself and returns home; Beauty comes to the world and goes forth to final victory. In his death as the Son of Man, Christ fulfills till the end his exodus from the Father and from self in freedom; and there, too, is prepared for him the paschal exodus of his return to the Father. On the cross, Beauty supremely happens: Beauty that came in the flesh tastes supreme abandonment and deepest communion.

When crucified Beauty is abandoned on the cross, we contemplate the infinite fragility of existence in the starkest manner: "My God, my God, why have you forsaken me?" (Mark 15:34). Jesus' cry at the ninth hour speaks of our fragility, with which he made himself one. No mystical notion of death can deprive it of its darkness, the wrenching mystery and drama of this apparently one-way exit from human existence on earth. In this sense, the death of the Crucified One really shows how the supreme abandonment experienced in death leads us to the very threshold of the deepest separation from our Origin, and so to the deepest wound. We die alone: loneliness is, and remains, the unavoidable price of our supreme hour: "I am deeply grieved, even to death; remain here and stay awake with me. . . . Could you not stay awake with me one hour? . . . My God, my God why have you forsaken me?" (Matt. 26:38, 40; 27:46). We die crying out as we did at our beginning, wounded then as now, proclaiming different kinds of birth: "We appear, we cry out: this is life; we cry out, we leave: that is death" (Auson de Chancel). Beauty abandoned on the cross reveals our deepest tragedy.

And yet the crucified Christ also shows us the loving face of the hidden Other: "Father, into your hands I commend my spirit" (Luke 23:46). The abandoned Son is in deep communion with the One who abandons him: he hands himself over, accepting the Father's will with loving obedience. The Father truly hands himself over, too: he does not spare his own Son (cf. Rom. 8:32). Jesus gives himself (cf. Gal. 2:20): he lives his death, the ultimate abandonment, as an act of freedom and of supreme acceptance. And so the cross shows that it is possible to be at once very far, and very near: the pain of the furthest separation is transformed by the fire of love, which is as strong as death (cf. Song 8:6).

To die in the Beauty that dies is "to abandon oneself" into God's embrace, letting everything be transfigured in him who welcomes us into another, new beauty. Beauty revealed on the cross reveals the littleness of the fragment, but also that it can be the place where we pass into the Mystery, thanks to the Son who came in the flesh once for all and made death his own. His death, the death of Beauty, opens the way for us to the impossible possibility of life, to the death of death, to the victory of ultimate Beauty over all that passes. . . .

Beauty That Will Save the World

Yet which of us can live like him, most beautiful of the sons of men, as in the hour of his death he draws communion and abandonment into one? Who like him can pass beyond the threshold? According to the faith of the New Testament, in the beauty of the Crucified One distance and intimacy meet, thanks to the Consoler's power: "When Jesus had received the wine, he said, 'It is finished.' Then he bowed his head and gave up the spirit" (John 19:30). As the Spirit supports the abandoned Christ in the hour of his mortal destiny, the same Spirit keeps him united to God, making him able for the supreme sacrifice: this is the insight expressed in images of the "Trinitas in Cruce," where the death of the Crucified One is presented as a revelation of the Trinity. The Father bears in his arms the wood of the cross, from which hangs the Son enfolded in death, while the dove of the Spirit mysteriously separates and unites the abandoned Jesus and the One who abandoned him (see, for example, Masaccio's *Trinity* in the church of Santa Maria Novella in Florence). Thus "Death has been swallowed up in victory. Where, O death, is your victory? Where, O death, is your sting? . . . Thanks be to God, who gives us the victory through our Lord Jesus Christ" (1 Cor. 15:54f., 57). God comes to us so that we may go to him:

> Lead me away by the hand, my eyes closed,
> with no goodbye to hold me longer
> among those I loved,
> the little things
> that made me live.
> Little did I think, Lord,
> this blossoming of shadows,
> this light flight of life
> in a glance's fragile mirror,
> would be so deep,
> nor that the world
> as it grew dark,
> might be so bright
> with unexpected beauty.[14]

Crucified Beauty leads us back to Beauty at the end victorious: beyond all the words spoken in history there is, and remains, the divine care, the hidden Beauty. At the end this Beauty will be all in all, and the whole world will be his home, and then his silence, more eloquent than any word, will enfold all things: "Love never ends" (1 Cor. 13:8).

"Then," writes Karl Rahner, "you will be the last word, the only word that lasts, never to be forgotten. Then, when in death all things will fall silent, and I will have finished learning and suffering, there will begin that

---

14. R. Barsacchi (1924-1996), *Le notti di Nicodemo,* con introduzione di F. Lanza (Palermo: Edizioni Thule, 1991).

great silence, where you alone will speak, the Word from eternity to eternity. Then will cease all human speaking; to be and to know, to know and to experience, will have become the same thing. I will know as I am known, I will sense what you have always said to me: yourself. No human word, no idea, will stand between you and me. You yourself will be the only word of jubilation, of love and of life, which fills every corner of my soul."[15]

To come before this ultimate beauty — the goal of Christian hope and promised vision — is the gift and challenge offered to the gaze of the those who believe, provided they look to the One who has crossed the threshold once and for all: Christ, the "beautiful shepherd," abandoned and risen, pledge and foretaste of glorious Beauty in his crucified flesh, offered for the Father and us.

Dostoyevsky witnesses to this in a unique way: in *The Idiot* he has the young nihilist Hippolite, dying of tuberculosis at only twenty years of age, ask prince Myshkin, a mysterious Christ-like figure, an innocent who suffers out of love for all,[16] the terrible question: "Prince, is it true you once said that the world would be saved by 'beauty'? . . . What kind of beauty will save the world?"[17] The young man's question comes from his personal experience of suffering: he knows that there will be no redemption for him in the sense of "a happy ending," magically removing the scandal of his pain: "What is in all this beauty for me," he says, "when every minute, every second I am obliged, forced to know that even this tiny gnat, buzzing near me in the sunlight now, is taking part in all this banquet and chorus, knows its place in it, loves it, and is happy, and I alone am an outcaste and only through cowardice have I refused to realize this until now!"[18]

This is why the Beauty that will save the world must be different from all our dreams and desires for easy harmony: only if God takes to himself the infinite suffering of a world abandoned to evil, only if he enters into the deepest darkness of human misery, only then suffering is redeemed and death vanquished. But this is precisely what happened on the cross

15. K. Rahner, *Tu sei il silenzio*, 6th ed. (Brescia: Queriniana, 1988), pp. 34f.

16. On Myshkin as a Christ-figure in Dostoevski, cf. R. Guardini, *Dostoevskij. Il mondo religioso*, 4th ed. (Brescia: Morcelliana, 1995), pp. 271-323.

17. F. Dostoyevsky, *The Idiot*, trans. Henry and Olga Carlisle (New York: New American Library, 1969), part 3, chap. 5, p. 402.

18. Dostoyevsky, *The Idiot*, part 3, chap. 7, p. 432.

of the Son. And so Christ is the truth that saves; more, he is the true alternative to all the supposed truths of reason and its proofs. And he is this precisely because he is crucified Beauty, the divine All in the fragment of human suffering.

Neither, though, as we look on this crucified Beauty, foretaste of eternity, do we forget, or turn from, this world's fleeting beauty, to which our hearts are bound, for this is the very beauty to which the eternal Son bound himself with bonds of indestructible love, taking our flesh to himself and sweating blood before the impending doom of death. As we look forward to ultimate Beauty, victorious over evil and death, we do not despise the dignity of the beauty of this passing world, which the Son made his own by becoming a human being. In his Incarnation, in giving himself up to death for us, he promised that the last word over all that exists would be a word of life, not death: in the resurrection of the Crucified One, there is room, too, for the resurrection — promised, awaited — of penultimate beauty.

So it is that Christians can live the "ordinary" days of their lives with hearts in celebration: the invocation and expectation of eternity, guaranteed to us in the risen Christ, are no condemnation of our present exile, but redemption and salvation for all things transfigured from within by love and faith in him. Once again it is the poetic voice that perhaps expresses this best, in the exceptional beauty of Joan Maragall's *Cant espiritual*.[19]

The beauty of all that passes is the threshold that opens out on the horizons of the Beauty that does not pass, which we foretaste in love, and invoke in faith. The Whole offers itself in the fragment; the fragment opens itself towards the Whole through the Beauty that will save the world. Eternity has entered time so that time may enter eternity. This is the essence of Christianity, its great and simple truth, as eloquent today as at the very beginnings of the Christian movement: the Beauty that will save the world is the Beauty of the "beautiful shepherd," crucified and risen for love of each and every single person, and of all.

---

19. The original, with Spanish translation on the facing page, is in the *Obra poética* of the great Catalan author (Madrid, 1984), vol. 2, pp. 185f.

What "Essence of Christianity"?

"Among recent philosophers there is no one to equal Feuerbach in taking such an intense interest in the question of God, even if he went about the task with an unhappy love."[1] It was thus that Karl Barth recognized in the book published by Ludwig Feuerbach in 1841 under the title *The Essence of Christianity*, a work of unique importance for theology, in which the adult reason of modernity measures itself against Christianity in the most far-reaching way possible. It was in Berlin during the winter semester 1899-1900 that Adolf von Harnack gave a series of lectures with the same title as Feuerbach's work. The lectures were subsequently published in various editions, and aimed at showing that the Christian gospel and modern reason could be reconciled in a mutually fruitful way. In 1938 Romano Guardini, distancing himself from both these thinkers, published a little book, again under the same title, in which he contrasted the abstraction and aridity of ideological reason with the unique truth proper to Christianity, arguing that Christianity's essence lies precisely in recognizing the truth not in something, but in someone — the person of Christ.

Even if from different points of view, these three texts sought to respond to the same question arising in the modern context: What is the essence of Christianity, its living center, its vital reference point, its pulsating heart, from which everything radiates and to which everything re-

---

1. K. Barth, "Ludwig Feuerbach," in *Zwischen den Zeiten*, 1927, pp. 11-33, then in *Die Theologie und die Kirche* (München: Kaiser, 1928).

turns?[2] Or, to use Guardini's words, aware as he was of the crisis of modernity, and thus careful to distinguish and separate the essence of Christianity from that modernity: "What constitutes the particular quality proper to Christianity alone, in which it finds its foundation and which distinguishes it from other religious possibilities?"[3] To answer these questions today calls for a clarification of the similarities and differences between the three studies and their three different ways of loving Christianity: Feuerbach's "unhappy love," Harnack's "tranquil love," and Guardini's "paradoxical love." From this comparative approach it will be possible to show why in this postmodern age it is "crucified Love" — as has been suggested in these pages, in the light of Jesus' threefold "exodus" — that lies most fully at the center and heart of the Good News.

Feuerbach's "Unhappy Love"

It is thus that Ludwig Feuerbach presents the structure and principal thesis of his book *The Essence of Christianity:* "In the first part I show that the true sense of Theology is Anthropology, that there is . . . no distinction between the divine and human *subject.* . . . In the second part, on the other hand, I show that the distinction which is made, or rather supposed to be made, between the theological and anthropological predicates resolves itself into an absurdity. . . . The first part is the *direct,* the second the *indirect* proof, that theology is anthropology."[4] The whole work is the

2. For a history of the expression "the essence of Christianity" cf. H. Wagenhammer, *Das Wesen des Christentums. Eine begriffsgeschichtliche Untersuchung* (Mainz: Matthias-Grünewald, 1973): this study traces the appearance of the term "substantia christianismi" from the Middle Ages to Protestant orthodoxy and of "essentia christianismi" from Meister Eckhart to pietism. The expression "Wesen des Christentums" seems to have sprung up among the German spiritualists, the pietists, and the theologians of the Enlightenment. For a critical revisitation of the different approaches of the twentieth century to the essence of Christianity in German-language theology, cf. the collective work *Das Christentums der Theologen im 20. Jahrhundert. Vom "Wesen des Christentums" zu den "Kurzformeln des Glaubens,"* hrsg. M. Delgado (Stuttgart: Kohlhammer, 2000).

3. R. Guardini, *Das Wesen des Christentums* (Würzburg: Werkbund Verlag, 1938; (Katholische Akademie in Bayern, München, 1984); Italian translation *L'essenza del cristianesimo,* 8th ed., trans. Manfredo Baronchelli (Brescia: Morcelliana, 1993), p. 7.

4. L. Feuerbach, *The Essence of Christianity,* trans. George Eliot (New York: Harper & Row, 1957), p. xxxvii.

incessant "repetition" of this thesis, at times expressed positively — the awareness of faith is nothing other than the self-awareness of man made an object to itself — and at times negatively — the division thus introduced into the subject produces evident and dramatic consequences.

Given this, one can understand why Karl Barth should have written of Feuerbach's "unhappy love" for Christian theology and, more generally, for its principal object, Christ. "Love," because in the general context of Feuerbach's thought he could not have offered higher praise than to recognize in Christianity the most complete expression of the human condition; "unhappy," because this complete presence of the human in Christianity is as it were schizophrenic, such that what ought to be nothing other than the self-awareness of the subject is presented as the unhappy awareness that emerges in the human being when presented with the divinity, which is conceived as transcendent and separate from the human being. In this way, the highest praise becomes the worst criticism; and theology, totally swallowed up by anthropology, is reduced to a lie, almost an incantation pronounced by the human intelligence and heart as they seek assurance from above.

The reflection on "religion in its agreement with the human essence" comes down to the thesis that "Consciousness of God is self-consciousness, knowledge of God is self-knowledge."[5] It requires no great effort to notice that this thesis is simply presupposed; no other proof for it is offered than obstinately employing it to explain the various aspects of Christian teaching: the concept of God and religion, Christ and the incarnation, prayer and miracles.

Who is God and what is religion for Feuerbach's *Essence of Christianity*? "God is the manifested inward nature, the expressed self of a man, — religion the solemn unveiling of a man's hidden treasures, the revelation of his intimate thoughts, the open confession of his love-secrets."[6] Consequently, "The divine being is nothing else than the human being, or, rather, the human nature purified, freed from the limits of the individual man, made objective — i.e., contemplated and revered as another, a distinct being."[7] According to Feuerbach, then, it is soon said why human beings give themselves to this kind of self-projection: "Love is God him-

5. Feuerbach, *The Essence of Christianity*, p. 12.
6. Feuerbach, *The Essence of Christianity*, p. 12.
7. Feuerbach, *The Essence of Christianity*, p. 14.

self, and apart from it there is no God. Love makes man God and God man. Love strengthens the weak and weakens the strong, abases the high and raises the lowly, idealizes matter and materializes spirit."[8]

In other words, the human spirit, crushed by its fragility and weakness, considers it opportune to idealize itself, to liberate its self-image from every possible limitation, from every fragility and misery, and to identify in this liberated self-image a superior object that may be taken hold of, a transcendent and sovereign God to whom to entrust the perception of its finitude and desire for self-transcendence. Thus it is that "God is the mirror of man."[9] "God's love for me [is] nothing else than my self-love deified."[10] "God is a tear of love, shed in the deepest concealment over human misery. . . ."[11] My self-projection, ably purified of all my limitations beginning with the deeply disturbing limitation of death, is where God is really born: "The interest I have in knowing that *God is,* is one with the interest I have in knowing that *I am,* that I am immortal. God is my hidden, my assured existence; he is the subjectivity of subjects, the personality of persons. . . . God is the existence corresponding to my wishes and feelings: he is the just one, the good, who fulfills my wishes."[12]

No different is the explanation that Feuerbach offers for the incarnation of the Word: "The Incarnation," he says, "was a tear of the divine compassion, and hence it was only the visible advent of a Being having human feelings, and therefore, essentially human."[13] Precisely because of this, though, the idea of the incarnation is for him a fundamental contribution to the story of human self-awareness, the revelation of the deepest truth: that man is God, and God is nothing other than man made an object to himself: "In the Incarnation religion only confesses, what in reflection on itself, as theology, it will not admit; namely, that God is an absolutely human being."[14] "For what God is in essence, that Christ is in actual appearance. So far the Christian religion may justly be called the absolute religion. That God, who in himself is nothing else than the nature of man, should also have a real existence as such, should be as man

8. Feuerbach, *The Essence of Christianity,* p. 48.
9. Feuerbach, *The Essence of Christianity,* p. 63.
10. Feuerbach, *The Essence of Christianity,* p. 105.
11. Feuerbach, *The Essence of Christianity,* p. 122.
12. Feuerbach, *The Essence of Christianity,* p. 173.
13. Feuerbach, *The Essence of Christianity,* p. 50.
14. Feuerbach, *The Essence of Christianity,* p. 56.

an object to the consciousness — this is the goal of religion; and this the Christian religion has attained in the incarnation of God."[15] But this very contribution is also nothing other than a product of man, totally human, nothing other than a flower sprung from our earth. "Out of the human nature, therefore, as it reveals itself through the heart, has sprung what is best, what is true in Christianity,"[16] which thus strives to realize its unfulfilled aspirations: "The fundamental dogmas of Christianity are realized wishes of the heart; — the essence of Christianity is the essence of human feeling."[17]

This relationship between man and God, or rather between man conditioned by his limitations and the self-projection by which he seeks to free himself from these limitations, is expressed in prayer: "Thus what is prayer but the wish of the heart expressed with confidence in its fulfillment?"[18] Far from being a relationship with the Other, prayer is just a pious mask held over the relationship between the self and what is deepest in man, with what he would like to be and is not, with what he thinks he is able to become by projecting the hidden aspirations of his heart in the form of invocation: "Prayer is the absolute relation of the human heart to itself, to its own nature; in prayer, man forgets that there exists a limit to his wishes, and is happy in this forgetfulness."[19] By praying, man makes himself his own God, builds himself an altar, and places himself upon it as his own idol, finally liberated from every misery, if not immediately at least potentially, according to his heart's aspirations: "In prayer man adores his own heart, regards his own feelings as absolute."[20] One thus understands why — for religion — everything is possible to prayer, even a miracle; a prayer, indeed, that did not presume the possibility of the miracle, would not reflect at all the most secret hopes of humanity, which is all the more ambitious, the more it is fragile and destined to death: "Miracle presents absolutely nothing else than the sorcery of the imagination, which satisfies without contradiction all the wishes of the heart."[21]

15. Feuerbach, *The Essence of Christianity*, p. 145.
16. Feuerbach, *The Essence of Christianity*, p. 60.
17. Feuerbach, *The Essence of Christianity*, p. 140.
18. Feuerbach, *The Essence of Christianity*, p. 122.
19. Feuerbach, *The Essence of Christianity*, p. 123.
20. Feuerbach, *The Essence of Christianity*, p. 125.
21. Feuerbach, *The Essence of Christianity*, p. 134.

The conclusion drawn from these arguments is the repetition of what has been affirmed since the start: "We have reduced the supermundane, supernatural, and superhuman nature of God to the elements of human nature as its fundamental elements . . . the beginning, the middle, and the end of religion is man."[22] As if this were not enough, however, Feuerbach proposes to strengthen his thesis by proving it beginning from its opposite, dealing with religion "in contradiction with the essence of man." As the projection of desire explains the birth of God and of his Christ, so the disappointment of unfulfilled expectations, projected into prayer but frustrated in reality, shows the unresolved split produced by religion, and Christianity in particular. Precisely the strongest faith is exposed to the greatest disappointment: Christianity is at one and the same time the sweetest intoxication of the heart and also its infinite, incurable frustration. The reason for this lies in the wound that man's self-projection inevitably involves: "Religion is the relation of man to his own nature, — therein lies its truth and its power of moral amelioration; — but to his nature not recognized as his own, but regarded as another nature, separate, nay, contradistinguished from his own: herein lies its untruth, its limitation, its contradiction to reason and morality."[23]

Religious experience thus issues in an unhappy, wounded, unfulfilled consciousness, because the distance created between the object of desire and the subject that expresses it is like a sharp blade inserted into the unity of the spirit, making the religious man into an alienated being, the slave of the result of his own process of abstraction, marked by his own permanently unmet need: "In religion man necessarily places his nature out of himself, regards his nature as a separate nature. . . . God is his *alter ego,* his other lost other half; God is the complement of himself; in God he is first a perfect man."[24]

In this sense, religion cannot but produce dependence and obscurantism: "God is the idea which supplies the lack of theory. The idea of God is the explanation of the inexplicable, — which explains nothing because it is supposed to explain everything without distinction; he is the night of theory, a night, however, in which everything is clear to religious feeling, because in it the measure of darkness, the discriminating light of the un-

---

22. Feuerbach, *The Essence of Christianity,* p. 184.
23. Feuerbach, *The Essence of Christianity,* p. 197.
24. Feuerbach, *The Essence of Christianity,* p. 195.

derstanding, is extinct; he is the ignorance which solves all doubt by repressing it, which knows everything because it knows nothing definite, because all things which impress the intellect disappear before religion, lose their individuality, in the eyes of the divine power are nothing. Darkness is the mother of religion."[25]

Feuerbach closes his reflections with this double affirmation: negatively, he affirms that "religion is a dream in which our own conceptions and emotions appear to us as separate existences, beings outside of ourselves";[26] positively, he insists that "the secret of theology is nothing else than anthropology."[27] His love for the Christian God remains "unhappy": to this God he concedes the merit of having revealed without a shadow of doubt that the divine and human coincide, from the moment that God became man. Yet, nevertheless, this God cannot but also be the cruel God who leaves unfulfilled the aspirations of the human heart: a God who — precisely as the self-projected essence of man freed from all chaff — places himself before human awareness as an unattainable mirage, a threatening, looming judgment beyond all proportion. Thus it is that, having wanted to prove "too much," *The Essence of Christianity* shows its weakness: if God is really a pure creation of man, and as such capable of being manipulated by human awareness, then it cannot be explained how at the same time this God can be both human desire and the denial of that desire, liberating self-projection and mortifying self-frustration. How can God, created by man, turn against his own creator, in a kind of upside-down repeat of Adam's sin!

Feuerbach's thesis thus remains without foundation, contradictory in itself. The fact that it is continually invoked in hammering repetition only demonstrates its weakness: "begging the question" — considering as the premise of an argument the conclusion that one seeks to prove — is never a good argument, even if one tries to impose it by repeating it *ad infinitum!* It thus seems to me that Feuerbach's "unhappy love" in the end shows itself to be the negation of itself in its contrary: neither true "love," nor truly "unhappy." It is not love, because we can only love what is other than ourselves: if God is only the man who creates him, then God will never be loved by the human heart, which, by loving in such a

25. Feuerbach, *The Essence of Christianity*, p. 193.
26. Feuerbach, *The Essence of Christianity*, p. 204.
27. Feuerbach, *The Essence of Christianity*, p. 207.

God nothing other than itself, would fall only into tragic selfishness! Nor can Feuerbach's love for the object of his thinking call itself truly "unhappy," because — not existing as love — it can neither exist as the pain of not being loved nor of not knowing how to love.

Indeed, Feuerbach's writing appears devoid of all the pain of love: his obstinate repetition of his thesis gives the impression of an operation of the intellect, full of itself, incapable of letting itself be called into question. What Feuerbach lacks is the perception of the Other in all his real otherness: in his work, it is the triumph of the subject that is celebrated, no more or less than in the more radical forms of idealism, which will be the matrix of all the ideological disasters and of their dramatic, totalitarian, and violent consequences. In this, Feuerbach is no more than another child of the Enlightenment, a consistent expression of adult and emancipated reason and of its pretensions. His Christianity is aligned with the ideals of modernity, of that rationality which claims to bless all things with the kiss of its light. The essence of Christianity, the absolute religion even according to Feuerbach's own definition, must be sought elsewhere. . . .

Harnack's "Tranquil Love"

If Feuerbach's love for Christianity is "unhappy," or perhaps, more precisely, falsely unhappy, Adolf von Harnack's is "tranquil." It lacks the fire of passion, the wound of suffering, the trial of paradox and scandal. Everything is reconciled in his religion of the interior life: faith and reason, God and man, Christianity and modernity. The world's adult conscience — which began maturing in the "century of lights" — can consider itself well served by this its heir, at once religious and critical, a man of faith and a rigorous historian, an "organic" intellectual and professor capable of suspicion and deep insight.

His lectures on the essence of Christianity — given in the winter semester 1899-1900 — are the distillation of an entire cultural world: the world of the late 1800s, liberal and bourgeois, thirsting precisely for that conciliation of which Harnack is the master. Optimism regarding progress — celebrated in the sumptuous galas of the "belle époque" — deeply pervades the words of the professor from Berlin, giving them an almost inspired tone, even — with hindsight — a touch of farce: "Jesus opens up to us the prospect of a union among men, which is held together not by any legal ordinance, but by the rule of love, and where a man conquers his enemy by gentleness. It is a high and glorious ideal, and we have received it from the very foundation of our religion. It ought to float before our eyes as the goal and guiding star of our historical development. Whether mankind will ever attain to it, who can say? But we can and ought to approximate to it, and in these days — otherwise than two or three hundred years ago — we feel a moral obligation in this direction. Those of us who possess more delicate and therefore more prophetic perceptions no longer regard the kingdom of love and peace as a mere Utopia."[28] It is like listening to the swan-song of an epoch on which the sun is already setting: and this sunset will be marked by Harnack himself in August 1914, when, with another ninety-three men of culture and art, he signs the "Manifest der Intellektuellen," giving assent and support to the belligerent policy of the German Kaiser.

Harnack's lectures did not in any way foresee the tragedy that would mark the century that was just beginning: on the contrary, the love that inspires him is entirely pacific, tranquil. The lectures are developed in two parts: "The Gospel" — organized into the three themes of the kingdom of God, God the Father with the connected infinite value of the human soul, and the highest justice represented by the commandment of love; and "The Gospel in History" — described according to the evolution of Greek, Latin, and German Reformed Christianity.

The questions underlying the lectures are these: "What is Christianity? What was it? What has it become?"[29] The chosen method is that of historical criticism: "What is Christianity? It is solely in its historical sense that we shall try to answer this question here."[30] Nevertheless, the rationalistic claim — according to which reason is the norm and final yardstick of every judgment — already makes its appearance in the programmatic intention "to grasp what is essential in the phenomena, and to distinguish kernel and husk,"[31] where the criterion of discernment of the one from the other is nothing other than the refined critical reason of the researcher!

28. A. von Harnack, *What Is Christianity?* trans. Thomas Bailey Saunders (New York: Harper & Row, 1957), p. 114.

29. Harnack, *What Is Christianity?* p. 6.

30. Harnack, *What Is Christianity?* p. 6.

31. Harnack, *What Is Christianity?* p. 12.

And yet, Harnack loves the object of his study, or, perhaps, he loves what he thinks about it; this is shown by the exaggerated way he praises it from the outset: "The Christian religion is something simple and sublime; it means one thing, and one thing only: Eternal life in the midst of time, by the strength and under the eyes of God."[32] Further on he will underline this enthusiasm several times: "Take the people of Israel and search the whole history of their religion; take history generally, and where will you find any message about God and the good that was ever so pure and so full of strength — for purity and strength go together — as we hear and read of in the Gospels?"[33]

Harnack's guiding idea is Christianity as a religion of the heart, in which God speaks to the soul and makes it beautiful in love: "Jesus never had anyone but the individual in mind, and the abiding disposition of the heart in love."[34] Even the social aspects of the faith are made to give first place to the interior life, attained and transformed by the proclamation of the advent of the kingdom of God: "The gospel is a social message, solemn and overpowering in its force; it is the proclamation of solidarity and brotherliness, in favour of the poor. But the message is bound up with recognition of the infinite value of the human soul and is contained in what Jesus said about the kingdom of God."[35] For Harnack, it is on this link to the interior life that the whole understanding of Christianity stands or falls: "The gospel makes its appeal to the inner man, who, whether he is well or wounded, in a happy position or a miserable, obliged to spend his earthly life fighting or quietly maintaining what he has won, always remains the same."[36] The only thing necessary thus consists in entering the kingdom of love, preserving precisely this gain "with tranquility," and this happens by conversion of the heart, which makes the individual a citizen of the kingdom. "He is forced to make himself a native of the kingdom of God, the kingdom of the Eternal, the kingdom of Love; and he comes to understand that it was only of this kingdom that Jesus Christ desired to speak and to testify, and he is grateful to him for it."[37]

The image of God that best corresponds to this primacy of the heart

32. Harnack, *What Is Christianity?* p. 8.
33. Harnack, *What Is Christianity?* p. 48.
34. Harnack, *What Is Christianity?* p. 111.
35. Harnack, *What Is Christianity?* p. 101.
36. Harnack, *What Is Christianity?* p. 115.
37. Harnack, *What Is Christianity?* p. 121.

and of its deep needs is that proclaimed by Jesus: God as father. "But in this case the message brought was of the profoundest and most comprehensive character; it went to the very root of mankind and, although set in the framework of the Jewish nation, it addressed itself to the whole of humanity — the message from God the Father. Defective it is not, and its real kernel may be readily freed from the inevitable husk of contemporary form. Antiquated it is not, and in life and strength it still triumphs to-day over all the past. He who delivered it has as yet yielded his place to no man, and to human life he still to-day gives a meaning and an aim — he *the Son of God.*"[38]

If God is the father, this means he is a God who loves, welcomes, and forgives, a God of mercy who heals the wounds of contrite hearts and fills with peace whoever turns to him with confidence: a God who reconciles opposites, overcomes resistance, brings contraries together. A God, who pouring love into human hearts, leads man to a measure of harmony and interior unity to which nothing and no one else could lead him: for Harnack, here lies the greatness of Jesus' message!

The romantic ideal of the beautiful soul, pacified in the divine and thus made a sharer of that kingdom of reconciled and pure souls which is the kingdom of God on earth, reaches its highest fulfillment in this interpretation of the gospel: the essence of Christianity — as Harnack perceives it — is the most adequate response to the desire of modern man, perceived in the depths of his heart thirsty for total reconciliation. And since, for adult and enlightened reason, the man who has reached full self-awareness is the emancipated man born with the age of lights, what goes well for this man goes well for human beings in general. To show the full power of the good news will mean showing how it is perennially up-to-date: "I have tried to show what the essential elements in the Gospel are, and these elements are "timeless." Not only are they so; but the man to whom the Gospel addresses itself is also "timeless," that is to say, it is the man who, in spite of all progress and development, never changes in his inmost constitution and in his fundamental relations with the external world. Since that is so, this Gospel remains in force, then, for us too."[39]

Harnack seeks confirmation for his interpretation of the essence of Christianity in the history of the effects that the gospel has produced in

38. Harnack, *What Is Christianity?* p. 130.
39. Harnack, *What Is Christianity?* p. 149.

time: a story of difficulties and distortions, in which, however, although the skin sometimes seemed to replace the fruit, it did not succeed in corrupting its essence. Thus it is that "The formation of a correct theory of and about Christ threatens to assume the position of chief importance, and to pervert the majesty and simplicity of the Gospel."[40] This corruption happens in the East as in the West: if the Greek church *"takes the form, not of a Christian product in Greek dress, but of a Greek product in Christian dress,"*[41] *"the Roman Church in this way privily pushed itself into the place of the Roman World-Empire, of which it is the actual continuation;* the empire has not perished, but has only undergone a transformation."[42] Certainly, among the many shadows lights are not lacking, as, for example, the West's Augustine, a true master of the interior life: "Up to the day in which we live, so far as Catholic Christians are concerned, inward and vivid religious fervour, and the expression which it takes, are in their whole character Augustinian. . . . Thus arose the astonishing 'complexio oppositorum' which we see in Western Catholicism: the Church of rites, of law, of politics, of world-domination, and the Church in which a highly individual, delicate, sublimated sense and doctrine of sin and grace is brought into play."[43]

The great return to the interior life will, though, only be achieved with the Reformation: "But no one can survey the history of Europe from the second century to the present time without being forced to the conclusion that in the whole course of this history the greatest movement and the one most pregnant with good was the Reformation in the sixteenth century . . . a religion without priests, without sacrifices, without 'fragments' of grace, without ceremonies — a spiritual religion!"[44] This is all owing to the German spirit: "From the time that the Germans endeavoured to make themselves really at home in the religion handed down to them — this did not take place until the thirteenth century onwards — they were preparing the way for the Reformation. And just as Eastern Christianity is rightly called Greek, and the Christianity of the Middle Ages and of Western Europe is rightly called Roman, so the Christianity of the Reformation may be described as German."[45]

40. Harnack, *What Is Christianity?* p. 184.
41. Harnack, *What Is Christianity?* p. 221.
42. Harnack, *What Is Christianity?* p. 252.
43. Harnack, *What Is Christianity?* p. 260.
44. Harnack, *What Is Christianity?* p. 268.
45. Harnack, *What Is Christianity?* p. 282.

From this very personal reading of history Harnack holds that he can derive a general law, which he considers valid always and everywhere: in every historical process, that which is and remains alive is the interior life. "Here, again, then, we are reminded of the fact that, so far as history is concerned, as soon as we leave the sphere of pure inwardness, there is no progress, no achievement, no advantage of any sort, that has not its dark side, and does not bring its disadvantages with it."[46] Thus Christianity resists, surviving all the incrustations that have weighed it down and hidden it: since its essence is the interior life of the soul that has been touched by the good news of God as Father and of his kingdom as kingdom of love, the sun of the gospel cannot set. "If we were right in saying that the Gospel is the knowledge and recognition of God as the Father, the certainty of redemption, humility and joy in God, energy and brotherly love; if it is essential to this religion that the founder must not be forgotten over his message, nor the message over the founder, history shows us that the Gospel has, in point of fact, remained in force, struggling again and again to the surface."[47]

The greatness of modern science and the miracles of progress will never be able to give what the Christian religion gives, because they remain external to the interior life of man: only the gospel of the love of God and of love of neighbor can speak to the heart and make it beat with the joy that never ends. "It is religion, the love of God and neighbour, which gives life a meaning; knowledge cannot do it. . . . But to the question, Whence, whither, and to what purpose, it gives an answer to-day as little as it did two or three thousand years ago."[48]

The impressive success of Harnack's lectures at the beginning of the twentieth century and for some decades later finds in these considerations its true reason: what he affirmed responded completely to the spirit of the age, expressed its aspirations, and sanctioned its optimism. Consecrating the sanctuary of the interior life, Harnack provided a justification for the widespread tendency of the European bourgeoisie to shut its eyes to the other side of the story, to those places where the old continent's "belle époque" was being translated into the most various forms of modern colonialism and imperialism, or where it found its bru-

---

46. Harnack, *What Is Christianity?* p. 187.
47. Harnack, *What Is Christianity?* p. 299.
48. Harnack, *What Is Christianity?* p. 300.

tal contrast in the very unjust social conditions in which the majority of society, also in Europe, was living.

A gifted thinker like Ernesto Buonaiuti, even despite his "modernist" sympathies, was able to express his sincere dissatisfaction for this reading of a dimension of the gospel and above all of history: "Harnack's lectures on the essence of Christianity, upon which I threw myself with a deeply anxious curiosity, disappointed me entirely. I found myself unable to recognize in that desiccated vivisection of Christian tradition anything other than the extreme fruit of Lutheran individualism and subjectivism, brought to their final consequences and the most dusty of dilapidations."[49] The same Buonaiuti, in two lectures given to the University Circle of religious studies in Rome in 1921, and published with the eloquent title *The Essence of Christianity,*[50] maintained that Harnack had condemned Christianity in the name of history, and that this was not acceptable. When, though, Buonaiuti tries to present the essence of Christianity and identifies it in an original ethic, enlivened by a luminous eschatology and warmed by a profound experience of salvation, he does not distance himself a great deal from the professor from Berlin. It remains true, though, that the individualism of the beautiful soul can be reconciled only with difficulty with the gospel preached by Jesus, who calls his disciples to live out among themselves a relationship of love analogous to that which he lives with the Father. The essence of Christianity cannot be another name for the modern triumph of subjectivity, even if consecrated with the most noble and pious of ideas about love: it must be sought in another and different direction. . . .

Guardini's "Paradoxical Love"

It is to these "modern" interpretations of the Christian faith by Feuerbach and Harnack that Romano Guardini seems to be offering a polemical response in his short work on *The Essence of Christianity:*[51] "The problem relative to the 'essence' of Christianity has been solved in various

---

49. E. Buonaiuti, *Pellegrino di Roma* (Bari: Laterza, 1964), p. 37.

50. Roma: Bardi, 1922.

51. Cf. R. Guardini, *Das Wesen des Christentums* (Würzburg: Werkbund Verlag, 1938; München: Katholische Akademie in Bayern, 1984); Italian translation by Manfredo Baronchelli, *L'essenza del cristianesimo,* 8th ed. (Brescia: Morcelliana, 1993).

ways. It has been said that this essence consists in the fact that the individual personality comes to occupy the central point of religious awareness; that God manifests himself as Father, and that the individual stands before him in a relationship of pure immediacy; that the love of neighbor becomes the decisive value and such like — up to the attempts to demonstrate that Christianity is the perfect religion, simply because it conforms to the maximum to reason, because it offers the purest morality and is in accord in the best way with the exigencies of nature. These answers are all mistaken."[52]

The error of the interpretations of Feuerbach and Harnack — which, though different, both remain perfectly in conformity with the order of reason, and so in a sense are still completely idealistic and liberal — consists above all in limiting the whole of Christianity to a part: interior life against exterior life; anthropology against theology; love against faith. The principal mistake, however, is another: "These answers are false for this reason — and this is the decisive element — that they are given in the form of an abstract definition, which reduce their 'object' to a general concept; but it is precisely this which contrasts with the deepest awareness of Christianity, because in this way it is reduced to mere natural premises: and precisely to that which experience and thought understand under the name of personality, religious immediacy, love, reason, ethics, nature."[53] Wanting to reduce the essence of Christianity to a general category, these efforts lose sight precisely of that which characterizes the Christian faith in its absolute originality, that which is irreducible to anything else and for which no analogy can be found.

The "Christian specific" cannot then be deduced from anything other than the unique, unrepeatable Christian revelation: "That which is Christian cannot be derived from worldly premises and its essence cannot be determined with natural categories, because this eliminates its peculiarity."[54] There thus emerges the key idea of Guardini's proposal: the Truth, which Christianity professes, is not something, but Someone, not an object that is possessed and measured in the context of the objects of this world, but the living person of Jesus Christ, who calls us to follow him and places each person before the decisive choice, which cannot be trans-

---

52. Guardini, *L'essenza del cristianesimo*, p. 8.
53. Guardini, *L'essenza del cristianesimo*, p. 9.
54. Guardini, *L'essenza del cristianesimo*, p. 10.

ferred to others. "Christianity is not a theory about Truth, or an interpretation of life. It is also this, but this is not its essential nucleus. This is constituted by Jesus of Nazareth, by his concrete existence, by his work, by his destiny — that is, by a historical personality."[55] We are Christians when we accept without condition the lordship of the Other over our lives, setting apart the modern myth of the absolute autonomy of the subject to accept the only dependence that makes human beings truly free: on the Mediator in whom God revealed himself. "Christianity affirms that because of the incarnation of the Son of God, because of his death and resurrection, because of the mystery of faith and grace, all creation is called to give up its — apparent — autonomy and to place itself under the lordship of a concrete person, that is, of Jesus Christ, and to make this person our own decisive norm."[56]

We can readily understand how this submission can appear paradoxical to adult rationality emancipated by modernity: "From the logical point of view this is a paradox."[57] Here lies the whole novelty of Guardini's proposal with respect to those of Feuerbach and Harnack: while they took modern subjectivity for granted as the norm and yardstick to which everything has to be referred, even the divine and the human experience of it, for Guardini the essence of Christianity consists in turning this premise radically upside down, so that it is not the human which is the measure of God, but the person of the incarnate Word who is the measure of the human being: "Christ in person is the decisive moment of salvation. Not his teaching, not his example, not even the power of God which works through him, but simply he himself, his person."[58]

Guardini's position has, in fact, far-off origins: it emerges in the context of the "modern" question of the truth, as this was posed by the Enlightenment. In the name of the absolute claims of enlightened reason, a distinction was introduced between contingent "historical truths" and universal and necessary "truths of reason," on the basis of which it seemed that Christianity, founded on the paradox of the incarnation of God, was deprived of every possible claim to absolute truth and consequently of every universal significance. The idea of a "universale

55. Guardini, *L'essenza del cristianesimo*, p. 11.
56. Guardini, *L'essenza del cristianesimo*, p. 12.
57. Guardini, *L'essenza del cristianesimo*, p. 12.
58. Guardini, *L'essenza del cristianesimo*, p. 36.

concretum et personale" seemed entirely inconceivable to modern reason: this was why Gotthold Ephraim Lessing had not hesitated to speak of the "accursed wide abyss" of the centuries, separating us from the historical Jesus, which can in no way be crossed, even by someone who — as he maintained to have done himself — had "often and with every effort attempted the jump."[59]

Against this suffocating embrace of modern rationality, claiming to understand and explain everything, Christian awareness had reacted in various ways: Søren Kierkegaard had responded in terms of the "singularity of the true." According to him, that which exists is never a simple "case" of the universal, nor a pure moment of the process of the eternal Spirit, but always and only an absolutely unique individuality, unrepeatable and not capable of being reduced by any totalitarianism whatever. In consequence, the truth is either free appropriation and interior life, which grows deeper through existing in the subject, or — simply — it is not.

United in their rejection of the claims of absolute reason, other Christian thinkers had sought an alternative response to the challenge of the moderns in the incontrovertible objectivity of the true: this was the approach of the Neo-scholastic school, which took up again the Aristotelian-Thomistic tradition concerning the equation of being and truth. There were, finally, some great spirits who reaffirmed the Christian claim to truth not in the name of singularity, or beginning from abstract objectivity, but through the conjugation, without mixture or confusion, of truth and history: to this group there belong thinkers like Johannes Adam Möhler, Antonio Rosmini, and John Henry Newman.

It is here that Guardini, too, is to be situated: convinced that the truth transcends reason, and that it cannot therefore be reduced to reason's overly narrow and short dimensions, he holds in consequence that the world of modern ideology — built exclusively on the possibilities of reason — cannot advance any absolute claim to truth. To reduce the essence of Christianity to the horizon of modern rationality, as do, even if in different ways, both Feuerbach and Harnack, is then an error. Neither, on the other hand however, can there be affirmed a presumed self-evidence of truth, excluding any historical mediation, because always and in any case the truth will have to make use of the language of human beings in

---

59. Cf. G. E. Lessing, *Über den Beweis des Geistes in der Kraft* (Braunschweig, 1777).

order to communicate with them. The truth, which is beyond history, cannot but pronounce itself in history if it wants to communicate itself to the minds and hearts of human beings in a way comprehensible to them. For the Christian faith, the story chosen by God to communicate himself to human beings is the story of Jesus of Nazareth, Lord and Christ: in it the truth happens, offering itself in the mediation of events and words, and thus placing each one of its interlocutors in the situation of a decision, by which it can be welcomed or rejected. "Everything that in the Christian sense comes from God to us — and equally everything that in the Christian sense goes from us to God — must pass through him."[60] "The 'way' in the Christian sense is the very person of Jesus Christ,"[61] who is also inseparably the truth and the life (cf. John 14:6).

Guardini is well aware that the consequence of this encounter with the truth made person is crisis, "the crisis towards which objective thought is impelled by the primacy of the personal, as well as the crisis of thought concerning the universal in general, towards which that thought is impelled by Christian reality."[62] Without this scandal, we cannot, though, even begin to grasp the essence of Christianity: Christ in person is the true and the good, the exclusive yardstick of when knowledge and action is true and just before God. "Christ is the content and the yardstick of Christian action in an absolute sense. The good in every action is him."[63] "Jesus Christ is the *Logos* and the Word of the universe, the original Word, the prototype of every entity — he is also the response to the aspiration to value and aim of the movement of love of the universe."[64] What is lacking in the interpretations of Feuerbach and Harnack is, then, scandal: in them everything is reconciled, everything subjected to the primacy of the human horizon. What instead for Guardini is the Christian specific, the center and heart of the Good News, is expressed in the paradoxical conviction that "the person of Jesus Christ, in his historical uniqueness and in his eternal glory, is in itself the category that determines the being, the action, and the theory of that which is Christian."[65]

60. Guardini, *L'essenza del cristianesimo*, p. 39.
61. Guardini, *L'essenza del cristianesimo*, p. 41.
62. Guardini, *L'essenza del cristianesimo*, p. 43.
63. Guardini, *L'essenza del cristianesimo*, p. 49.
64. Guardini, *L'essenza del cristianesimo*, p. 74.
65. Guardini, *L'essenza del cristianesimo*, p. 77.

The Truth of "Crucified Love"

What Guardini has to say about the essence of Christianity certainly establishes a non-negotiable reference point, which can in no way be neglected. And yet his proposal, too, moves within the horizon of modernity, which is and remains the interlocutor of his polemical message; above all, he was responding in the context of the totalitarian and violent ideologies that he experienced in a concrete and personal way. Jesus Christ is affirmed by him as the truth in person, the concrete and personal universal, in precise and strong antithesis to the absolute claims of national socialism, in a way not dissimilar from that in which Karl Barth, drawing up the manifesto of the confessing church alternative to the regime, had thus affirmed at the beginning of the Declaration of Barmen: "Jesus Christ, as he is witnessed to us by Holy Scripture, is the only Word of God, which we must listen to and which we must trust and obey in life as in death. We reject the false doctrine, according to which the church as source of the Word's proclamation, may and must recognize, beyond and besides this unique Word of God, yet other events and powers, figures and truths as the revelation of God."[66] The anti-ideological power of these words is obvious: in this lies their strength, but also, to some extent, their weakness, which Barth himself recognized after the war when he wrote: "To say *no* is not in the end the highest point of art, to throw down idols cannot be our highest task."[67] These words are clarified by the declaration made a little later: "The fact remains that (while being 'joyously ready for battle') I have acquired more and more understanding for the great affirmations which the human being needs to *live* and to *die*."[68]

Guardini, too, is aware of the limitations of his own albeit vital assertions regarding the essence of Christianity, and he makes no mystery of this: "If Christ is the category of Christian thought, how do we receive the contents of this thought? How is the Christian affirmation constructed? The problems are extraordinarily difficult, and it appears that theological thought has not yet really embraced them with its gaze."[69] The "no" to the theses of Feuerbach and Harnack is complete, very

---

66. *Theologische Erklärung von Barmen* (May 31, 1934), quoted in *Die kirchliche Dogmatik*, II/1 (Zürich: Evangelischer Verlag, 1940), p. 194.

67. K. Barth, *Die kirchliche Dogmatik*, III/3 (Zürich: Evangelischer Verlag, 1950), p. ix.

68. Barth, *Die kirchliche Dogmatik*, III/4 (Zürich: Evangelischer Verlag, 1951), p. ix.

69. Guardini, *L'essenza del cristianesimo*, p. 79.

clear: if even for Guardini Christianity is "the religion of love," this love can be understood neither "as love in the absolute sense," according to Feuerbach's interpretation — human, only human — nor "as religious love in an absolute sense," according to Harnack's intimistic and conciliatory approach. The love of which Christianity speaks is "the love that is directed to Christ, and through Christ to God as also to other human beings."[70] This said, though, the question remains: "What does it mean to carry out, in love for Christ and through him, the different moral duties, which also must embrace existence with all its situations and realities and with all its values? How can the great variety of actions, which must build the world, be founded in love for Christ?"[71]

Leaving these questions open, Guardini shows that he is aware that his understanding of the essence of Christianity certainly affirms its universal truth, recognized in the person of Jesus, but in such a general way as to make it difficult to perceive the demands of the concrete, humble following of Christ: for him, too, it was easier to say the great "no's" and to affirm the great "yeses," than to pronounce the little, everyday "yeses" that human beings need in order to love and to die. Precisely in admitting this limitation, Guardini confesses his dependence on his polemical interlocutor, modernity, with its claims to absolute and total rationality: even he belongs to the world of Feuerbach and of Harnack, even if by rejecting it! And yet, precisely in recognizing his limitation, Guardini launches a program for the times to come: he seems to suggest that when the ideological moment is passed, when strong reason has expressed all its potential both for good and for evil, we will have to return to what is down-to-earth, to the humility of the works and days of individual human beings. And then universal truth — identified in the person of Christ — will have to be brought close to the weakness of the protagonists of real history, to

---

70. Guardini, *L'essenza del cristianesimo*, p. 79.

71. Guardini, *L'essenza del cristianesimo*, p. 80. Very close to Guardini's position — to which he frequently refers — is the Catholic theologian Michael Schmaus in his *Vom Wesen des Christentums* (Westheim bei Augsburg: Wiboradaverlag, 1947), in which he gathers the lectures from a course given at the University of München for students of all the Faculties in the winter semester 1945-1946. Schmaus attempted to find reasons for meaning and hope in the Christian faith after the tragedy of the Second World War. He seeks his answer in the person of Christ, historical revelation of God the Trinity and of man, the latter called to respond to divine love with love, and thus to live in the church the experience of communion that conquers loneliness and the absence of hope.

their suffering, to their loneliness. Then, when human beings are tempted to give up loving and they doubt whether it is possible to give meaning to life and history, we will have to say in a different way the same truth Guardini perceived as the center and heart of Christianity: the truth as it is revealed in the strength of the Almighty, but in the weakness and abandonment of the Crucified One.

It was to this "weak" truth, which lets itself be recognized in the countenance of the suffering God, that the American Protestant theologian William Hamilton wanted to witness in the book — with its deliberately provocative title — *The New Essence of Christianity*,[72] which appeared when the protest movements of the 1960s were beginning to gain strength (1966). Faced with the crises of the strong systems of modernity, for him the fragment is the only possible way to approach the truth, and thus also the only way available for a theological thought that wants to grasp the essence of Christian truth. In the age of the so-called "death of God," Hamilton believes faith has no alternative: either it goes on talking of the security offered by the omnipotent and impassible God, and thus is meaningless for human beings today; or it accepts as its yardstick the scandal of the suffering and death on the cross of the Son, and thus is able to understand "tragic humanism," which today characterizes the human condition, as it emerged from the century of world wars, of genocide and totalitarian systems.

The suspicion Hamilton harbors towards a faith that is too facile and consoling leads him, however, to conclusions that seem to constitute a surrender before the responsibility of serving the truth: "to be a Christian today is to stand, somehow, as a man without God but with hope. . . . Faith is, for many of us, we might say, purely eschatological . . . a cry to the absent God."[73] Since, though, the Crucified One made this very cry his own, it is in him that we can recognize a new image of God, a God who speaks to our hearts and helps us find reasons for life and hope. More than an affirmation of the truth, the essence of Christianity, which is understandable today, is for Hamilton an appeal to follow Christ, who in humiliation has revealed the lordship of God.

The doubt remains whether such an act of will will be enough to furnish a sufficient anchor for those who have been shipwrecked by

---

72. W. Hamilton, *The New Essence of Christianity* (New York: Association Press, 1966).
73. Hamilton, *The New Essence of Christianity,* pp. 63-64.

postmodernity. This is suggested by the rather limited role Hamilton assigns to the resurrection of Christ — which for him consists in "making present and available to men of faith the form of Jesus' lordship as a form of humiliation and suffering"[74] — and his draft for a Christian lifestyle, such as "can be both described and lived" without the confession of the Lord Jesus.[75] This is why Hamilton's study, while pointing to a real need, stops too soon, without reaching the specific of Christianity, that which Guardini had rightly perceived in the person of the Son made flesh. The weakness of the Christian God cannot thus in any way signify that he is unreliable, incapable of offering a sure destination for searching faith: the real problem to be faced is thus not the weakness of the One abandoned on the cross, but rather the possibility and the way of recognizing in this weakness the strength and wisdom of divine love for human beings. In reality, only when we recognize "crucified Love" in the abandonment of the Son will there shine out the closeness of the faithful God, not in spite of, but precisely beginning with this weakness, to which omnipotence consigned itself for love of humankind. And only then will crucified Love be seen as Good News, which enlightens and warms, which comforts and regenerates. "Crucified Love" will then offer itself in all its measureless human and divine depth as the gospel for this postmodern age, not as a "new" essence of Christianity, but as *that* essence, which from the beginning of the Christian movement has sounded out as Good News, and which we too, protagonists and heirs of the postmodern shipwreck, need in order to love and to die: the word of the cross.

74. Hamilton, *The New Essence of Christianity*, p. 116, n. 34.
75. Hamilton, *The New Essence of Christianity*, p. 122.